Volume 1

Genealogical Patterns:
Form & Meaning

Book 3: Meaning

MATERIALS FOR THE STUDY OF

SOCIAL SYMBOLISM
IN ANCIENT & TRIBAL ART

A RECORD OF TRADITION & CONTINUITY

Based on the Researches & Writings of

CARL SCHUSTER

Edited & Written by

EDMUND CARPENTER

Assisted by

LORRAINE SPIESS

ROCK FOUNDATION

1 9 8 6

Drawings By

MIGUEL COVARRUBIAS

KATHLEEN BOROWIK

FRANCES BRITTAIN

Designed By

SAMINA QURAESHI

AILEEN WINTER

Art Assistant

SUZY KITMAN

Readers

SCHUYLER CAMMANN

MARK SIEGELTUCH

TOBIAS MOSTEL

Unlimited thanks to numerous colleagues,
curators, archivists & correspondents who, between 1930–1985,
contributed time & thought to these volumes.

Volume 1

Genealogical Patterns:
Form & Meaning

Book 3: Meaning

Published by the Rock Foundation
Copyright © 1986 by the Rock Foundation, New York
Library of Congress Catalog Card Number 85-63003

ISBN 0-937691-03-8
ISBN 0-937691-06-2

Typography & Printing by Meriden-Stinehour Press
Printed in the United States

Contents Volume 1

Caduveo pencil drawing,
presumably of body-painting,
collected at Nalike, Matobrono,
Brazil, December 1935, by
Claude Lévi-Strauss, and sent
to Carl Schuster, 3.9.54.

In 1952, Schuster outlined the meaning of genealogical patterns in a lengthy essay entitled 'Genealogical Patterns in the Old and New Worlds', published in São Paulo in 1958. It had about as much impact as a wet sponge hitting Mont Blanc. The only comment came from Claude Lévi-Strauss in his Huxley Memorial Lecture, 1965:

'If social anthropologists were half as interested in material culture as they ought to be, they would probably have paid more attention to Carl Schuster's fascinating survey of the world-wide occurrence of a type of geometrical pattern which, from its geographical distribution and from known early examples, he thinks goes back to paleolithic times. These patterns are best understood when compared with kinship diagrams not unlike those used by modern anthropologists. Let us recall that in Australia and Melanesia, natives have been actually observed making such drawings. If Schuster is right, not only the facts of kinship, but the theory as well, may be scores of thousands of years old. What we have painstakingly unearthed beneath the facts might be nothing else than this age-old theory'*.

The rest was silence.

* Lévi-Strauss, 1965, p. 15.

That is, until recently. Now recognition is coming to Schuster, mostly from scholars in other fields. When I sent a copy of 'Genealogical Patterns' to Leo Steinberg, the art historian, he replied: 'Though I began reading with great resistance in the conviction that the author was wildly overinterpreting, I found myself gradually yielding, wooed over by the man's integrity and intelligence, and finally won over by the sweep of his imagination. In short, I am writing to tell you that you bestowed a great gift on me and that you created a fan. I only wish I had known the essay ten years ago. Now I find myself lamenting the fact that Schuster is no longer living. A strange sentiment, for I never mind learning that Einstein is dead, or Humboldt, or Paracelsus. But with this man there is so much I'd like to discuss. The knee alone, for example. It happens that I have a large file . . .'.

'I find the bent knee used as a thrusting member in rape scenes both in Hellenistic antiquity and again, far more explicitly, from the 16th century onward, eg Titian's *Tarquin and Lucrece*. Is this an irrelevant accident, or do those Renaissance masters of body language revert to an archaic tradition?'†

‡ Personal communication, 12/21/77.

FRANCOIS CARYPYRA.

Posts

923

98

The painted house-post in 923, made by Tukanoan-speaking Indians of the north-western Amazon basin, is decorated primarily with a genealogical pattern. Essentially the same pattern can be seen on a Carajá paddle, 98 (with zigzags & dots), and on a Guiana pottery bowl, 8.

The importance of 923, for the elucidation of 98 & 8, lies in the context in which it occurs. For here the genealogical pattern forms the body of a human figure whose head appears at the top, surmounting a spinal column in the form of a vertical bar. Presumably it was from such a composition as 923, dominated by a human head, that decorations like those of 98 & 8 were abstracted.

The pattern of all three designs derives from series of headless, spineless human figures joined by their outstretched arms & legs. The missing heads & spines are then represented collectively by the single large head at the top and by the central spinal column.

8

But this is not all we can learn from 923. Its design explains the persistent headlessness of figures composing typical genealogical patterns. For if we regard each conventionalized body in 923 as representing an individual, then these bodies collectively form the body of the tribe, for which there can logically be but one head—that of the tribal ancestor at the top of the pattern, through whom all individuals of the tribe are ultimately related.

So the design in 923 is far more than mere decoration: it symbolically represents the whole tribe.

Beyond this, the application of a genealogical design to a house-post is in itself significant. When we speak of an outstanding individual as a 'pillar of society', and when we speak of a family as a 'house', we are perpetuating metaphors which may go back ultimately to actual usage.

I think 923 represents such a usage, surviving in the tradition of a people closer to symbolic origins than ourselves. Not only figuratively, but literally, the tribal ancestor is here the pillar of the house, its physical strength being metaphysically reinforced by the strength of all the individuals forming the collective body of the tribe.

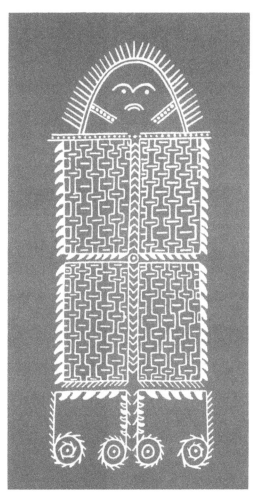

923

Spinal Columns

Genealogical patterns often emphasize spinal columns. But in 923, the spinal columns are extracted from their places and magnified into a single feature of dominant importance. The chevrons representing the vertabrae run in opposite directions from a central point, determined by a transverse bar and evidently conceived as an umbilicus.

If the repeating pattern represents the tribe, its divisions by this means into four equal sections probably refers to social divisions within the tribal body. Among the Cubeo, and presumably among other Tukanoan tribes, this would mean exogamous phratries or sibs. The spinal column thus appears to be a symbol of cleavage, not so much within the body of each individual, as within the body of the tribal ancestor, and thus conterminous within the body of the tribe.

The crossing of the spinal column by a horizontal bar suggests that the body of the tribal ancestor was conceived as divided into four parts, which must forever be reunited by individual marriages between members of the exogamous divisions in order to perpetuate the social fabric of the tribe.

A New Guinea myth tells of a god's body divided at its navel into four parts, from which all humanity descends[66]. Similar myths occur in other parts of the world. In them, the umbilicus serves as an omphalos or cosmic navel, by which the bodily divisions of the ancestor are aligned with the cardinal directions—an alignment ideally perpetuated in the relative geographical locations of the sibs or phratries comprising the tribe.

Simultaneously, the post embodying the ancestor represents the World Pillar or *axis mundi* supporting the firmament, as symbolized in the microcosm of the house roof (cf 3:1).

Two Melanesian House-posts

In the local art style of the Admiralty Islands, the painted ovals on the shaft of 334 represent headless human figures. Each is divided vertically by two parallel rows of dots representing the spinal column, as in 65, another Melanesian design. Zigzags connecting the points of these ovals represent common arms & legs in the same way as undulating bands connect ovals in 65, and spines in 3, likewise from Melanesia.

This characteristic Admiralty pattern differs from standard genealogical patterns in one respect: instead of being connected by common limbs, tiers of figures are separated by horizontal cross-bars. Its design symbolizes, I believe, a finite number of generations, rather than the endlessness of the genetic process implicit in more truly characteristic genealogical patterns.

Nevertheless, these generations of headless figures are all 'animated' at the top by a single, large head symbolizing the ancestor from whom they descend. The multiplication of bodies was probably conceived as strengthening the post symbolically. Shaft & capital together represent the inseparable, all-powerful unity of the tribe.

65

3

As for the zigzags carved in 173, a New Caledonian door-post or *tale*, these continuous limbs connect series of rudimentary human figures, the way undulating bands connect skeletal bodies in 3. Diamonds formed between the zigzags (or more probably star-shaped cut-outs within these diamonds) represent headless bodies. Each bank of zigzags (limbs) serves the bodies above & below. Again, the large head spanning the top of the post belongs to all the headless bodies comprising the shaft.

However obvious this explanation appears when a typical New Caledonian *tale* is aligned comparatively with other posts, it has not always been obvious to those who regard the study of New Caledonian art as an exclusive regional specialty. Sarasin, Leenhardt & others agree that the *tale* represents an ancestor, but are at a loss to explain its 'geometric' pattern. In what appears to be an indirect quotation from a native informant, Compton comes closest to the mark when he describes the lozenges as 'stomachs', using the plural, of the figure whose head forms the capital[67]. Sarasin writes that 'such a repetition, though in itself senseless, would not be contrary to the laws of design'[68]. What is really senseless is the invocation of imaginary laws of design to explain forms best understood by comparison with phenomena outside the limited area under consideration.

173

1184

Tupinamba Warrior

A document of prime importance for this phase of our study is the tattoo on a Tupinamba warrior, *1184*, as recorded by Claude d'Abbeville, a Capuchin missionary in the 17th century. This design differs from that of *115*, a Tukanoan house-post, only in the absence of bars and the multiplication of stepped lines.

According to d'Abbeville, *1184* represented to its wearer and to his compeers, a record of the twenty-four enemies whom he killed in battle and whose names he acquired[69].

The Tupinamba, then, recognized the elements composing this pattern as human figures. Since the basic meaning of all such patterns is genealogical, is there a connection between Tupinamba ritual homicide and the idea of tribal continuity which might explain the use of this pattern as a record of human sacrifices?

I think there is. In Tupinamba ritual, the body of the slain captive was first quartered, and its parts assigned to various individuals to be eaten. This assignment was, for the participants, a matter of great social importance[70]. All of which suggests the ritual re-enactment of a widespread creation myth, according to which the human race is descended from the dismembered parts of a primordial body, with certain peoples, tribes or sibs descended from certain parts, in geographical alignment with the four quarters.

This idea may be read between the lines of a remarkable speech made by a captive warrior before his execution[71]. In accordance with a formula customary on such occasions, he taunted his tormentors by claiming that in eating him they would eat their own relatives & ancestors, since he had earlier eaten of these when they fell captive to his own people.

This diatribe should be considered in conjunction with the fact that not only the executioner but all the male & female relatives of his generation changed their names when the victim was executed. His death thus symbolized a whole generation's rebirth, and his sacrifice was somehow associated with the tribe's perpetuation.

When the Tupinamba captive proclaimed his 'honor' at being dismembered & eaten, this was not only bravado, but reflected the knowledge, or at least vague memory, that in this grim drama he was impersonating the ultimate ancestor, and was thus virtually a god, or God Himself, whose body was to be consumed in a communion.

That the Tupinamba executioner (who was often the son of the victim's captor) did not himself partake of the victim's body may be explained in the light of the Mexican practice, according to which captor & captive acknowledge their relationship to be symbolically that of father & son, and the captor abstains from eating of the sacrificed captive specifically for this reason[72].

The general relation between Tupinamban & Mexican cycles of captive-sacrifice and cannibalism has been pointed out by Radin, who also noted that the Tupinamba regard each captive enemy as a substitute for one of their own dead[73]. Like the Mexican captive, the Tupinamba captive was treated, until his sacrifice, as a god; but also as the equivalent of an ancestor in the sense of a dead relative.

When he applied a genealogical pattern to his body to commemorate the slaying of captives, the Tupinamba warrior also commemorated his own genealogy in terms of ritual sacrifices.

115

13 Houses & Dancers

Social Body

The human form assigned to posts &
houses is often that of the Ultimate Ancestor. Whether this ancestor is represented by a living dancer or an immobile
house-post or even by the house itself,
matters little: the symbolism is the same.
Society and the human body are conceived
as mirrors of each other: the Ultimate
Ancestor incorporates all of his descendants, who are the tribe; and his body
parts, in turn, represent the divisions of the
tribe.

A creation myth from the Society Islands
explains how the architecture of a house
literally 'embodies' Ta'aroa, the First
Ancestor, who was dismembered to create
the world: 'Ta'aroa was a god's house; his
back-bone was the ridge-pole, his ribs
were the supporters'[74].

To the residents of such a house, the
meaning of the ancestral house-post is
often primarily *social*. But where the
ultimate ancestor is conceived as God, that
function becomes *cosmic*. Thus the
Tikopia of Polynesia regard the house-
post as a demi-god who provides communication between this world and the
macrocosm[75].

Both as First Ancestor and as Cosmic Pole
the center-post serves as a means of
communication with forces beyond. Not
all such posts bear genealogical patterns,
but among those that do, some are said to
provide a means of rebirth, permitting the

soul to ascend through successive generations until reunion is achieved with the
First Ancestor. This basic notion underlies
'heavenly ladders' (cf 2:9), as well as
cosmic games played on the body of a
primordial giant (cf 3:6–8). It applies
particularly to sacrificial posts where
captives, forced to impersonate ancestors,
are sacrificed & buried. More remotely, it
appears in the myth of the virgin who
embraces a center-post or Tree of Life, and
thereby conceives a son destined to found
a tribe or perform miracles.

Lévi-Strauss describes Northwest Coast
Indian house-posts as 'less things than
living beings' who, in days of doubt &
torment, guide the inhabitants, comfort
them and indicate the path out of their
difficulties[76]. A 'refinement' of such ideas
may exist in the caryatids of the Athenian
Erechtheum.

Each clan in a Papuan men's house has a
division assigned to it and regards the
anthropomorphic post or posts of that
section as belonging to the clan; but the
central post has relation to the whole
house & tribe[77].

In a Sumba house, one pillar, called the
'oracle post', stands out as 'exceptionally
important'. Ancestral spirits, believed to
come from Heaven to listen to appeals, are
consulted here daily. Like the roof, this
post is carved & sacred; both are closely
associated with spirits[78].

1185

Tukanoan House

Tukanoan social ideas are symbolized architecturally in a variety of ways. Each rectangle in the checkerboard facade of *1185* represents a dancing-costume with fringes at the bottom, similar to the typical Tukanoan house-post, *923*. The heads of the wearers of these costumes (perhaps conceived as masks) are represented in a frieze of alternately dark & light faces at the top, just under the overhanging roof.

I see this facade as a genealogy representing the enlarged family which figuratively constitutes the 'house'. I assume the reciprocal coloring of the heads & bodies refers to the warp & weft of the tribe's social fabric. If so, these alternately dark & light heads may simply represent male & female partners in the family structure—or, by extension, exogamous clans.

When Koch-Grünberg photographed *1185*, the inmates of the house posed before it in two groups: men & boys on one side of the door, women (and presumably a girl-child) on the other side. Koch doesn't tell us whether he asked them to pose in this way. It seems more likely they simply acted in accordance with custom.

923

1186

Dogon House

Consider *1186*, the facade of a Dogon house in West Africa. According to a Dogon spokesman: 'The front wall with its eight rows of ten niches . . . represents the eight ancestors and their descendants, numerous as the fingers on their hands.

'In the vertical direction the two series of five columns are the ten fingers, and when one looks at the front of the house one sees hands spread out. The niches are the homes of the ancestors, who occupy them in the order of birth beginning with the highest row'[79].

When contemplated at a distance, Dogon granary doors look 'geometrical', eg *1187*. But the human figures composing them are identifiable. To the Dogon, they represent mythical ancestors and their numerous descendants. Griaule & Dieterlen tell us that *1188* summarizes the principal mythical events which both preceded & followed man's creation. They also illustrate the first four lineages (representing the first four tribes of the Dogon) and the first three mythic generations[80].

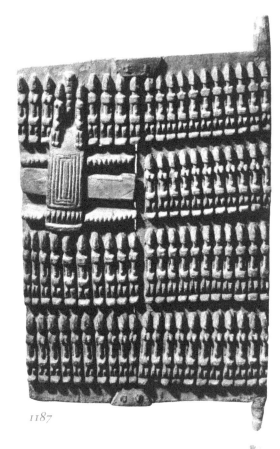

1187

1188

Colombian Pilasters

Each pilaster in certain tombs in the Cauca
valley of Colombia has a human head for a
capital, as well as a genealogical pattern
on its shaft, 1189 . Enough is left of the
original limbs to indicate the design's
derivation from series of interlocking
human bodies, highly simplified, as in 173 .

How accurately this tomb decoration
reflects the domestic architecture of the
people buried there, I don't know. Even if
these decorations imitate beams &
matting, this doesn't exclude a symbolic
explanation; the two reinforce each other.
I regard these pilasters as genealogical in
the same sense as the Tukanoan house-
posts, and their lattice decorations as
comparable to decorations on Tukanoan
dancing-costumes and those of their
neighbors, eg 921 .

173

921

1189

Argentine Columns

A stone column or menhir found at Tafí
in Tucumán province, northwestern
Argentina, *1190*, presumably was set up
as a free-standing memorial. But it conforms to the formula of a post with a
human head for a capital and a genealogical pattern on its shaft. On *1190*, this
pattern was rendered vertically, but the
same design may have been applied to
movable objects as well and been biaxial,
like so many other South American
designs. Seen from the side, the raised
parts form series of human bodies separated by engraved lines; seen vertically, the
design is an excerpted band from a pattern
of linked circles.

Another stela at Tafí, *1191*, bears a more
conventional genealogical pattern, similar
to a petroglyph in the Argentine
Territorio del Rio, *1192* (modified into a
continuous-line drawing).

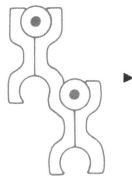

1190

1191

1192

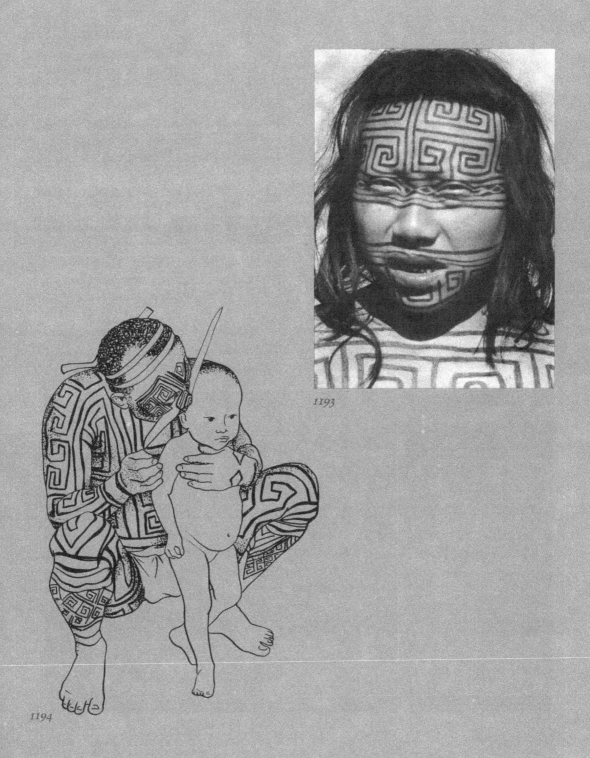

1193

1194

Both designs have their analogy in the living art of tropical forest Indians far to the north: in the body-painting of two Kashinawa, *1193 & 1194*, both from Peru; and in a Carajá dancing-costume, *107*, from Brazil.

107

Peruvian House-post

Consider  1195, a house-post from eastern Peru. The rectangular space just under its carved capital contains a rudimentary face: a nose with attached eye-brows—an interpretation supported by more naturalistic house-posts from the same region, eg 1196.

Tessman long ago surmised that the 'geometric' designs of eastern Peru, of which 1196 is typical, derive ultimately from human figures[81]. I agree. I see 1196 as a genealogical pattern—highly evolved & simplified—from series of connected human bodies.

1195   1196

923

115

The fact that this pattern reaches up to the nose, apparently covering the mouth, may find its explanation in body-painting. For house-post patterns are also painted or tattooed on bodies. Thus typical house-post patterns, eg 923 & 115, were painted not only on dancing costumes, but directly on bodies, for festive occasions[82].

Where patterns used in body-painting & tattooing are themselves composed of series of conventionalized bodies, their application to the body makes the wearer into a living image of his tribe. This corresponds to the conception of the anthropomorphic house-post as a composite tribal spirit. Whether the body-decoration was copied from the house-post or the other way around need not concern us: in either case the design is a 'tribal' pattern in the sense that it repre-sents the tribe as a composite of all its members.

Not all patterns used by South American Indians for body-decoration necessarily derive from series of linked human figures. But some do, and a considerable number may ultimately be explained in terms of genealogical symbolism.

Dancers

Speaking of the Tikopia of Polynesia, Firth tells of seeing several women during a ceremonial cycle and being told, 'The Atua Fafine (chief Goddess), it is she'[83]. For all his efforts, he fails to make this sound logical to Westerners who regard several as plural and 'she' as singular. But in genealogical patterns: One is Many; Many, One.

Tikopian house-posts are sometimes conceived, though not represented, as deified ancestors. In particular, the central-post of a temple 'is under the control of the main deity of the temple– "it obeys him"; it is spoken of as his post, and it is even ritually treated as his "body"'. His descendants are known collectively by the name of the ancestor's 'house'[84].

In a periodic rite of renewal, a 'dancing-skirt' is tied around the 'body' of this Tikopian post-god. This fact helps us to understand 923 as a dancing costume with a fringe at the bottom. Presumably among the Tukanoans, as among the Tikopians, the ancestor god of the post was once conceived as the first dancer or the initiator of the dance.

This may also explain a Himalayan custom, at royal weddings, of tying white scarves around specific pillars on the palace grounds to honor those pillars as 'the chief support of the house'[85].

923

1197

Many tribesmen conceive of houses as extensions of their bodies. They 'wear' houses, the way they wear tattoos & clothes. Posts & houses imitate body-decorations & clothing; body-decorations & clothing, in turn, imitate posts & houses.

Bacairí dancers in Brazil wear grass costumes sometimes so large they look like thatched roofs, eg *1197*, and are, in fact, called 'houses'[86]. The dancer is thus, so to speak, an animated house-post, or the house-post is an immobilized dancer. Here the dancer, like the house-post, represents the First Ancestor, who introduced the dance.

Bacairí dance-masks, and those of neighboring tribes on the upper Xingú River, eg *1198*, are sometimes decorated with a genealogical pattern extending just up to the level of the eyes. Though this design looks merely decorative, it is a *Biaxial System* composed of crossed hourglass figures with extended arms. Normally such a system was placed on the torso. Here it was transferred to the face or mask because the body, in dancing, was covered by a grass costume.

The Bacairí name for this design, *mereschu* (a kind of fish caught in a net) was accepted literally by von den Steinen, just as Müller interpreted Maglemose hexagonal patterns as representing fishnets[87]. Both designs resemble nets, but I doubt that either was designed as such.

The Bacairí name has about as much value as any 'popular etymology' has for the linguist: namely *nil*. A distant analogy is more rewarding: among the Boroko of West Africa, a net-like mantle, representing a genealogical pattern, is placed around the torsos of male initiates[88].

1198

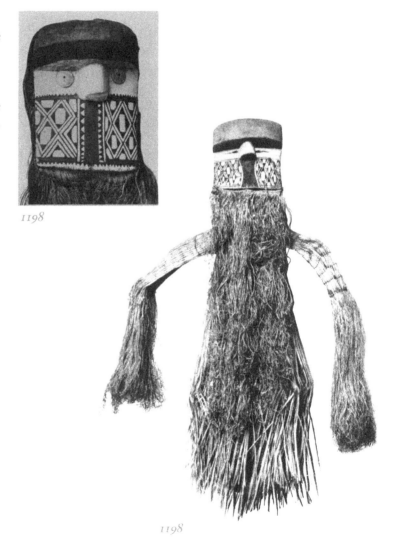

1198

1199

1200

Mehinacú Indians of the upper Xingú construct anthropomorphic posts, eg *1199 & 1200*, each with a genealogical pattern covering its torso, a human head and two dancing sashes. Oberg provides a detailed description of this ceremony, called *kwarúp*, among the neighboring Camayura. The posts, he reports, represent the four original ancestors, as well as more immediate ancestors deceased during the previous year. Posts are cut from the sacred *camuva* tree, out of which the first ancestors allegedly came and whose wood is otherwise reserved for ritual objects and center-posts.

At the *kwarúp* ceremony, the dead are mourned and youths are initiated into marriage. Marriage in the presence of the dead is a symbolic act, intended to perpetuate *&* increase the tribe. The Camayura say that, if they do not perform the *kwarúp*, the tribe will die out[89].

Transferred Patterns

115

Just as 1184 was tattooed only on the
torso, exclusive of the arms & legs (those
parts, namely, which were cut away if the
warrior was captured!), so there is no
representation of limbs in 115: they were
apparently 'thought away', as if unfit to
carry the pattern. And in corresponding
dance-costumes, eg 921, the genealogical
pattern is painted only on the torso, while
the arms are hidden by sleeves (a surprising accessory in the jungle!), and the legs
by a fringe, which reappears in conventional form in 923.

Whatever may be the meaning of these
correspondences, they show a close relation between body-painting, dancing-
costumes, house-posts & memorial-
columns.

Perhaps the most striking similarity
between 1184 & 115 is the obliteration of
the lower part of the face by an upward
extension of the body-pattern. In 1197,
this peculiarity is understandable: no
other space is available. But in other cases,
eg 1184, this obviously doesn't apply. I
offer no explanation.

923

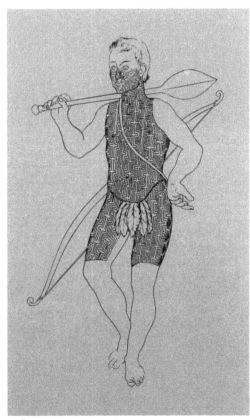

1184

1197

Thus genealogical patterns, though primarily applied to the trunk of the whole body, were sometimes extended beyond it. In certain cases, they persisted in these transferred locations after they disappeared from the body itself. An instance of this may be seen in designs painted on the arms, and apparently only on the arms, of certain Caduveo women of southern Mato Grosso, an excerpt of which appears in *116*. Structurally, *116*, *1184* & *115* are the same, though crossbars are lacking in *1184*.

116

The impulse which prompted the Caduveo women (or their ancestors) to apply *116* to their arms probably was the same as that which prompted the Tukano, Tupinamba and perhaps several other South American tribes to apply similar designs to their trunks. All these designs are but variants of a single type, evolved from series of human figures joined by their outstretched limbs and symbolizing the principle of descent or pedigree. Their use for body-decoration expresses the wearer's pride in his tribal connections. Among the Caduveo, the application of this pattern to the upper arms is restricted to women of 'noble' ancestry[90].

Today *116* is worn only on the arms; conceivably it once covered the body, or most of it. A pattern of headless human figures makes sense only if these figures are animated by the head of a living person who wears the pattern. And conversely, the only type of pattern which really makes sense as a body-decoration is one composed of headless bodies.

921

14 Continuous Limbs

.

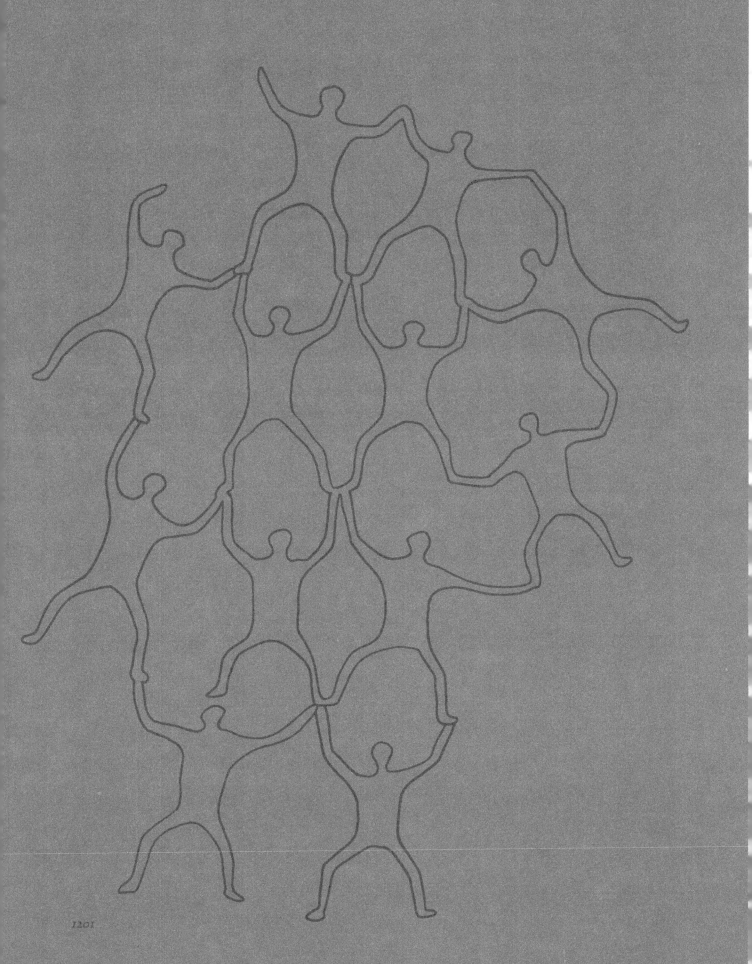

1201

Australian Creation Ritual

What distinguishes genealogical patterns from mere representation of human figures is the continuous limbs. These can only be symbolic; nothing like them exists in nature. And what they symbolize can only be familial & social connections.

Direct evidence confirms the great antiquity of genealogical patterns. The ideas behind these ancient patterns are more elusive. But there are indirect means of penetrating the barrier closed by history: in the customs, beliefs & rituals surviving among the Australian aborigines lie plausible solutions for some of the enigmas posed by the art of our earliest ancestors.

Figures *1201–1203* show the outlines of earthworks prepared for an initiation ceremony in 1894 by the Kamilaroi tribe of New South Wales. Mathews reports that the 'life-size' men in *1201* 'were formed by cutting a nick or groove in the ground along the outline of each'; and that 'all the figures were joined together, the hands and feet of one joining the hands and feet of the others'[91].

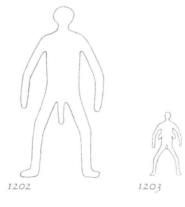

1202   *1203*

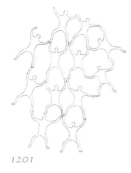

1201

The Kamilaroi told Mathews that *1201* 'represented the young men who were with Baiamai at his first camp'. Baiamai, the Creator of the Kamilaroi, was himself shown, not as part of the connected group, but separately as an earthen figure of heroic proportions (about 4.5 meters long), *1202*, opposite his consort, Gunnanbeely, carved in life-size, *1203*.

Mathews continues: 'They say that Baiamai created them (the Kamilaroi) and gave them the country and all that was in it for their use, after which he and Gunnanbeely went away. A short distance from [*1202 & 1203*], the figure of a man and woman were formed on the ground behind a tree and were partly hidden. The blacks said that these represented their original parents, whom they called Boobardy and Numbardy—meaning father and mother respectively'. (This pair of figures is not reproduced by Mathews. Perhaps they were represented *in coitus*.)

What do we make of these explanations? All seek to explain a complex of ideas centering around the theme of *creation*. This theme is represented first, by the images of the Creator-pair, *1202 & 1203*; second, by the pair of figures called 'father' & 'mother', whom the Kamilaroi evidently regard as their more immediate ancestors; and third, by the composition which chiefly concerns us, that 'of the young men at Baiamai's first camp', *1201*.

The relation of *1201* to the other figures is somewhat obscure. Yet I suppose that 'the young men who were with Baiamai at his first camp' were the first figments of his creation or the first human beings, and thus ancestors of the Kamilaroi. Perhaps they were the progenitors of various tribal subdivisions.

Mathews wasn't told why the figures of *1201* were joined together by their limbs & feet. But the meaning of connected limbs in general emerges in the light of another ritual observed & recorded elsewhere in Australia some forty years later.

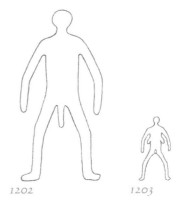

1202   *1203*

Cape York Ritual

In 1935 Ursula McConnel described &
photographed a ritual she observed
among the Wikmunkan & Wiknatara
aborigines on the western side of Cape
York Peninsula, in northwestern Australia, *1204* & *1205*. This ritual was performed by 'a line of men lying on the
ground . . . with hands clasped. One in the
middle represented a baby [made of bees-
wax] lying on her abdomen. Those on the
left of the "woman" are men who are
growing old. Then came woman and
birth. Those on the right are the children
who came after the result of sex and birth.
At the end of the line stands a man who
swings the *moipaka* [bullroarer, female].
The ritual symbolizes the continuity of life
by means of sex and birth'. The author
adds: 'It must be realized that the spiritual
power behind this ritual is believed to be
invoked by its performance and to bring
about the desired continuity of life. Hence
its sacred character'[92].

There are differences between *1204* &
1201: in *1204*, men in a single line join
hands; in *1201*, figures spread in all
directions, joined leg-and-arm. Yet both
arrangements illustrate essentially the
same idea: creation & procreation. What
the Kamilaroi represent statically in art,
the Cape York aborigines enact in ritual.

1204

1205

1204

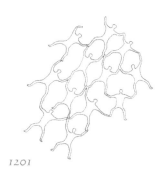

1201

120

If clasped hands symbolize genetic continuity in *1204*, does this same meaning apply to the common limbs of *120*, a painted skin robe from this same part of Australia? Note the *Shadow System* of two interlocking *Type 1* genealogical patterns. Both are composed of reptile-like human figures, a familiar motif for representing ancestors. Unfortunately, no record survives of the artist's intention.

The importance of the Kamilaroi pattern, *1201*, is that it came to the attention of observers able to transmit to us at least an inkling of its ritual meaning to its makers. I assume some such ritual is also depicted in *179*, a Spanish cave painting, circa 4th millennium BC. Both arrangements are noteworthy for their irregularity: in neither are the figures joined in a rigidly repeating pattern.

The Australian figures are connected by their limbs, but in one case a leg rests on the head of another figure (lower left in *1201*). This may be the exception which proves the rule of ligature by limbs. I suspect that ligature by the head, which occurs in several places in *179*, is the result of accident or carelessness, and that the correct connection is by limbs.

The Australian figures in *1201* represent males; the Spanish figures in *179* probably represent females, with the exception of the male figure at the lower right. In *1204*, all the performers are men; even the central parturient woman is impersonated by a man. This may simply be a consequence of male monopoly of ritual. Or this all-maleness could be associated with the *couvade*. Female impersonation could explain the single male figure in *179*.

A 'female' bullroarer, *1205*, is swung in this ritual as a symbolization of the genetic process and as a prayer for continuation.

1205

179

1206

1207

Today in Arnhem Land, initiates still wear painted genealogical patterns, eg *1206*; and during their initiation, still lie side-by-side, eg *1207*. Note the joints rendered as dark dots. Spines are rendered as columns of white dots in the second figure from the bottom in *1207* and in *1208*, a painted wooden figure from this same area.

1208

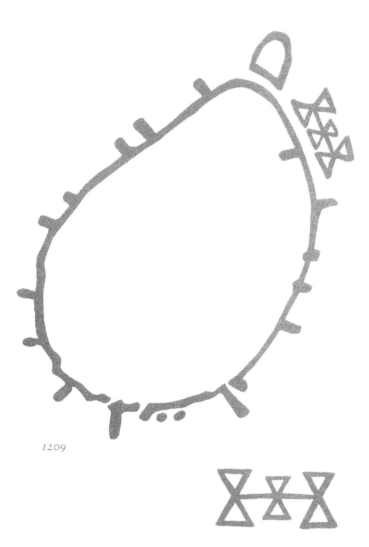

1209

North American Creation Ritual

Remarkably similar rituals occurred among a desert people in southwestern North America. In the late 19th century, Bourke published an account of a dance which the Mohave said represented their myth of creation: 'Where the big medicine man representing the Judge (the Creator) was to stand was marked this [1209], and near this on the ground was traced a hieroglyph, the meaning of which [his informant] was unable to give, but which bore some slight resemblance to the figures of a man, woman, and a child or of three grown persons tied together'[93].

What the Mohave drew were classic hourglass figures from a reciprocal pattern. Like the Kamilaroi earth-images, these were scraped in the ground and, again like the Kamilaroi images, explicitly associated with a creation ritual. Bourke makes no mention of any Creator-pair or parental-pair comparable to the Kamilaroi images. But such earth-images exist in this general region.

On both sides of the Arizona-Sonora border, monumental sculptures were made in prehistoric and possibly proto-historic times by scraping surface stones away to outline effigies and other forms[94]. Two male figures lie near Ft. Mohave, Arizona, 1210: below the 'right' elbow of the man with the head occurs a third, smaller figure, lacking sex features.

1210

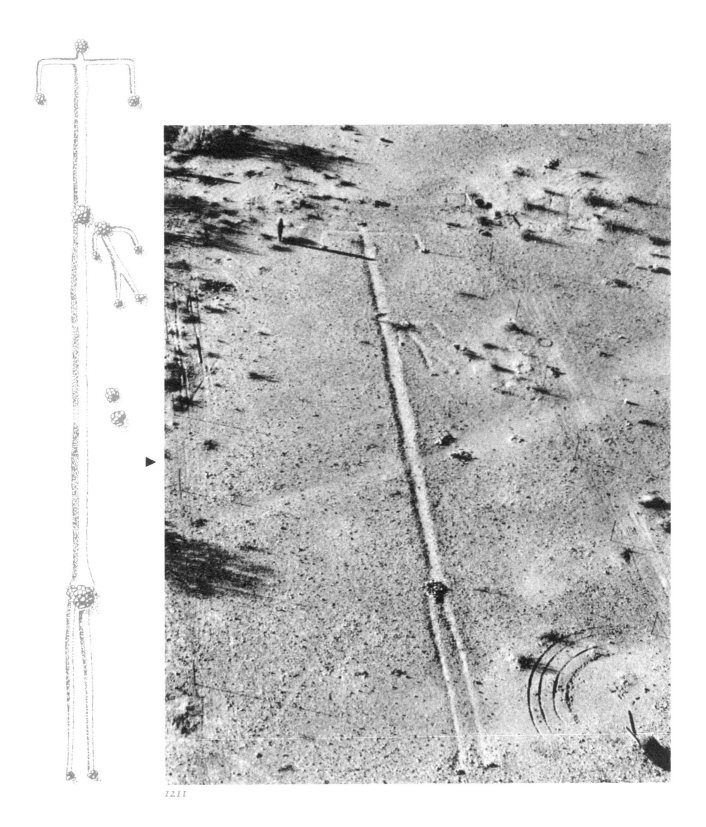

1211

Near Sacaton, Arizona, a human form (54 meters long) lies beside a second figure (4.5 meters long), *1211*. A nearby pair of earth figures, *1212*, repeats this difference; and so do two South Dakota stone figures, *1213*, one male, the other female.

Paired earth-figures, one large, the other small, have an enormous distribution in the Old & New Worlds. Where distinct sexual differences are absent, their 'male' & 'female' natures can usually be inferred from their relative sizes and other characteristics.

Perhaps only among Australian tribes is their original conception, as 'the first man and his wife', still alive or was alive until recently. Descendants of American Indians who constructed paired earth-figures don't speak of them in precisely these terms. Yet their ancestors may have done so. I suspect that in America, as in Australia, such male-female earth-monuments represented the original tribal ancestors in 'primordial copulation', the monument being the point of origin of the tribe and, by extension, the beginning of the world.

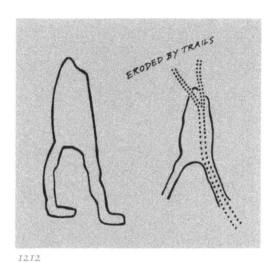

1212

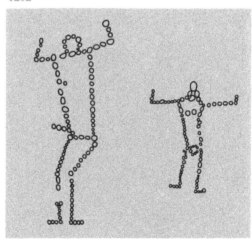

1213

15 Birth from Limbs

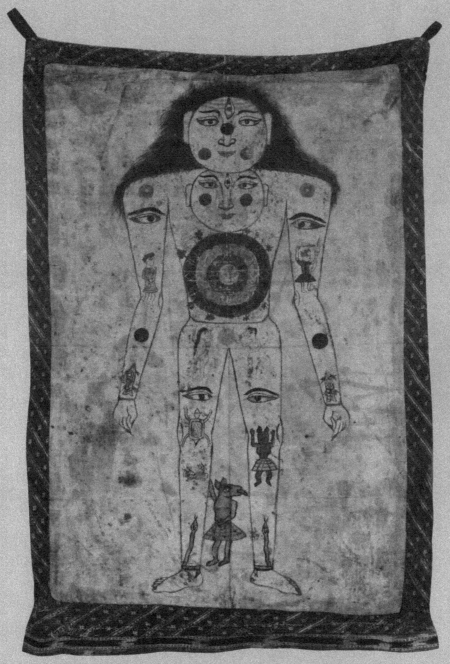

1225

Buds

Common-limbs *&* clasped-hands serve as bonds between generations not only in art *&* ritual, but in other traditions as well. Widespread myths tell of human beings born from limbs—sometimes from arms or fingers, more commonly from legs, and most commonly from knees. Those born in this way are generally described as 'the first people'; and the limbs from which they spring are said to be those of the Ultimate Ancestor.

African myths referring to birth from the knees or legs range from east-central Africa southward to the Hottentot[95]. A Masai story begins: 'There was once an old man who had no wife and lived alone in his hut. One night he went to sleep and when he awoke in the morning he found his knee (*gungu*) was swollen. There was nobody there to look at it, so he kept quiet thinking he had a boil. After waiting for six months he asks himself in his heart why the boil does not ripen so that he can break it. He waits two months more and, finding that it will not ripen, he fetches a knife and says, "Even if I die, I will break it", and he stabs it with the knife and out come two children'[96].

Association of the knees with generation occurs among the Yami of Botel Tobago, an island off the southern tip of Taiwan[97]; in Micronesia among the Marshall Islanders[98]; in the Finnish epic of the *Kalevala*[99]; and in at least one Indo-European cosmogonic legend[100]; not to mention the Greek myth of the birth of Dionysos, god of fertility, from the thigh of Zeus[101]. The theme was current among the Carib Indians of the Antilles[102], and survives among the Choco & Uitoto of Colombia and the Umutina of Brazil[103].

An Indonesian account tells of a man and a woman sealed in a tree trunk, which lands at Gunung Lubunut. There the woman gives birth to twins: a boy from her right calf, a girl from her left calf. Their offspring are forbidden to marry[104].

In northern Japan, there is a widespread folktale of the birth of a tiny boy from the swollen knee of an old woman, or sometimes of an old man. In Iwate prefecture, the boy, Sunelo-Tampako, 'Knee-Split', is reputedly born from the knee of an old woman who prayed with her husband for a child and was instructed by the Boddhisattva *Kwannon* to smear saliva (symbolizing semen?) on her knee.

A variant tale from Sado Island, Niigata prefecture, tells of a bean-sized boy born from the swollen finger of his childless mother. The diminutive child of these folktales generally transforms himself into a handsome youth who marries a heroine and brings wealth & happiness to his aged parents[105].

In a widespread Japanese folktale, the boy Momotaro is born from a peach, *momo*, which in Japanese also means 'thigh'. An Ainu tale concerns a hero, Omu-taro, born from the thigh (*omu*) of his mother. In a variant of this myth, the boy emerges from the heel of his mother after an ogress has devoured the rest of her body[106].

A Jakun (proto-Malay) legend speaks of the first woman 'whose children were produced out of the calves of her legs'[107]. In a tale from the Polynesian island of Mangaia, the boy Rongo came from a boil in his mother's arm, when it was pressed[108]. A New Guinea myth tells of two children born out of the blood of a woman's arm[109], while another tells of two sons born from the blood of a woman's finger[110].

Tales about children born from hand-knuckles occur among at least three ethnic groups in the Mountain Province of Luzon, including the Ifuago[111]. In another Philippine tale, miraculous birth takes place from *between* the fingers, rather than from the knuckles—presumably a rationalization of knuckle-birth, in which the cavity between the fingers is equated with the womb[112].

All such tales are of interest in connection with the genetic role of fingers and the related custom of reckoning kinship on fingers, as well as tattooing human figures on finger-joints. They also help explain the custom of sacrificing finger-joints in mourning for deceased relatives.

For each instance cited here, more can be cited for surrounding areas. However much these myths vary in details, they have a basic relationship to each other: birth from knees or legs is generally preceded by swelling of the affected parts, analogous to normal pregnancy. Sometimes a male child springs from the right knee and a female from the left knee, or different races or social subdivisions spring from the two knees, or from inside & outside of the knees.

These stories often appear grotesque to the point of absurdity: yet their vast distribution, perhaps throughout every continent, makes them impossible to dismiss as meaningless.

The Australian ritual at Cape York, *1204*, together with genealogical patterns generally, explain these stories and are, at the same time, explained by them. The conception of limbs as bonds connecting generations goes back thousands of years in art. It should hardly surprise us, then, to encounter this idea in tales & legends all over the world, especially in those purporting to explain the origin of humans. The vagaries of these legends might be likened to the conventionalizations of genealogical patterns.

Which came first: the idea or the image? Perhaps they came together, for man thinks in images. Often it's hard to explain the idea of 'genetic potency of limbs' except by reference to a genealogical pattern. Conversely, it's hard to explain a genealogical pattern except by reference to the basic idea behind it.

1204

1214

Plants & Limbs

The analogy between the branching of plants and birth from limbs, especially from fingers, probably played a role, from the beginning, in furthering this belief in the potency of limbs. In Indo-European and many other languages, it survives today in that community of words shared by men & plants: trunk, limb, branch, sprout, bud, etc, as well as in the identical nomenclature for human joints and the joints of the stalks of plants.

It also survives in legends explaining human generation in terms of the propagation of plants. Thus the Hawaiian goddess Haumea, described as having 'a breadfruit body, trunk and leaves', allegedly produced the tribe of Pele from her dismembered parts[113].

The Batak drawing in 1214 shows a tree with a 'human trunk'. Presumably it depicts the sacrifice (by means of blow-guns) of a human victim tied to a pole—a sacrifice undertaken in the interests of fertility, the idea being that a 'cosmic tree' would sprout from the limbs & head of a buried corpse, 1215.

In the Naga Hills of West Turkestan, trees serve as skull-racks, eg 1216. Young branches grow directly through human skulls.

A modern drawing from Buka, in the
northern Solomons, *1217*, depicts 'The
old man from Bekut', and illustrates the
origin of trees and cultivated plants, as
well as the origin of the social order: those
growing to the right belong to the paternal
parents; those growing to the left, to the
maternal parents.

1216

1217

1215

1218

1219

1220

Conceivably this same symbolism underlies *1218*, a Mexican cut-out figure of a
'witch', though I know of no supporting
evidence for this. Similarly, I have no cor-
roborative evidence for including here
1219, an ancient grain-bin from Israel,
inscribed *&* painted with what looks like a
split *Count System* of hourglasses *&*
ramiforms. But the New Hebrides figures
in *1220 & 1221* are specifically identified
by their makers as ancestral figures and the
growths at their shoulders are said to be
more immediate ancestors of these
ancestors.

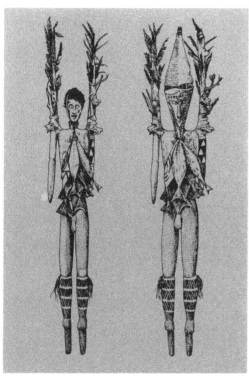

1221

1222

A myth current along the north shore of New Guinea relates how two heroes, apparently conceived as 'the first man' and his nephew, built a canoe carrying 'all the animals' to sea. They used for lashing the 'drawn-out sinews and blood vessels of the arms and legs of his [the nephew's] mother'. Then, somehow, 'men and women sprang from the cut off ends of these lashings' and proceeded to populate certain islands, which are duly enumerated[114].

Thus the woman's progeny sprang from her limbs, the way plants spring from the cuttings of a parent stalk. In fact, earlier in this story, her arms & legs are described as having the thickness of a tree and producing yams[115].

Certain South American pictographs & petroglyphs, eg *1222*, represent a figure (sometimes clearly female) presumably excerpted from a repeating pattern. Its limbs end in a multiplicity of lines, like the genetically potent 'drawn-out sinews and blood vessels of the arms and legs' of a procreative mother[116].

This gruesome and apparently nonsensical story makes sense when referred to figures joined by their arms & legs in a genealogical pattern. The 'mother' in this story is, as it were, excerpted from such a pattern.

1223

Origin of the World from the Limbs of a
Primordial Ancestor

Legends about birth from limbs can be
explained as fragments of a cosmogonic
myth, according to which the world in
general and mankind in particular origi-
nated from the parts of a primordial giant.
Myths of this type are found among tribal
peoples in many parts of the world,
though not necessarily among the same
people who tell stories about birth from
limbs.

Society Islanders say the Supreme Being
made the world by metamorphosis of
parts of himself: 'He took his spine for a
mountain ridge, his ribs for mountain
slopes, his vitals for the broad flowing
clouds, his flare and his flesh for fatness of
the earth, his arms and legs for strength of
the earth; his finger-nails and toe-nails for
scales and shells for the fishes, his feathers
for trees, shrubs, and creepers, to clothe
the earth; and his intestines for lobsters,
shrimps, and eels for rivers and seas; and
the blood for Ta'aroa got heated, and
drifted away for redness for the sky and
for rainbows.

'But Ta'aroa's head remained sacred to
himself, and he still lives, the same head on
an indestructible body'[117].

The same theme is illustrated in the art of
the nearby Austral Islands where the sea-
god Tangaroa, *1223*, is depicted in the 'act
of creating the other gods and man'.

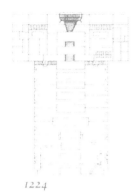

1224

Old Chinese lore includes a primal man known as P'an Ku. When he died, according to one account, his head formed the mountains, his eyes made the sun & moon, and the hairs on his head & body made the trees & plants. Another account says that his crying made the rivers, his breath the wind, his voice the thunder, and his glance the lightning—as though he were still alive.

'Tradition tells us that when Prince Yen, afterwards the Ming Emperor, Yung-lo, first arrived in Peking in the early 15th century AD, an eminent astrologer, Liu-Po-wen, gave him a sealed package which contained the lay-out of the new capital, to be called *No Cha*. These plans were based on the most approved principles of geomancy and allotted a certain building or open space to each part of the human body'[118].

In *1224*, *No Cha's* head & ears are represented by the *Chien Men* and its flanking gates; his limbs & organs by various buildings; his wind-pipe by the 'Imperial Way'; his navel by a well; his large intestine by an open gutter; etc.

Such accounts are also commemorated in the literature of early Indian civilizations. A Vedic hymn explains the origin of the world and of man from the parts of such a cosmic being (the *MahāPurusha* or Great Man), who is sacrificed and presumably dismembered for this purpose. The four primary castes of the Indian social system

are said to derive from the body of this being as follows: 'The Brahmin (priest) was his mouth, his two arms were made the Kshatriya (warrior), his two thighs the Vaisya (trader and agriculturalist), and from his feet the Sudra (shopkeeper and artisan) was born'[119].

A Jain image of this Cosmic Man, *1225*, has such warriors on his arm, while male & female figures on his thighs repeat the common theme that male & female children spring respectively from the right & left thighs.

Two Hindu myths belong to this series. The celestial Damsel (*apsaras*) Urvasi is said to have been born from the thigh of the male sage Narayana; and the Brahmans are said to have 'churned' King Prthu and Lady Archis from the arms of the tyrannical King Vena, after he had been killed by the curses of his oppressed subjects. Since all Indian kings are traditionally members of the Rajanya or Kshatriya caste, the latter story corresponds to the Vedic 'birth' from this caste from the arms of the Cosmic Man or *MahāPurusha*.

Though the joints of the limbs are not specifically mentioned in these Hindu accounts, the knees in particular play an important role in a popular variant of the same theme which survived until recently in the unwritten literature of Russia. *Poem on the Profound Book of Mysteries* explains various features of the physical world as parts of the body of a primordial Cosmic Being. In some versions, parts of the body of 'Adam' (a Christian substitute for this more abstract cosmic figure): the tsars from his head, the boyar-princes from other, unspecified parts of his body, and the peasantry or common people 'from the holy knee of Adam'.

Schayer shows that this poem relates not only to the Vedic *Purushasukta* but to variants surviving in the written literatures of various eastern peoples[120]. The generative function of the knees in this Russian poem is presumably an archaic trait, inherent in the prototype from which all of these legends descend. Schayer was himself aware that this type of myth, familiar to him chiefly in Indo-European & Semitic literatures, had relations to the oral traditions of 'Austro-Asiatic and Oceanian civilizations'.

Actually, its relations are wider. All these widespread stories about birth from the knees or legs ultimately relate to such cosmogonic myths as fragments to a whole. The basic myth of creation by dismemberment is much older than any of the literatures in which it was first recorded, and lies at the bottom, or very near the bottom, of all the phenomena studied here.

In formal literary traditions this cosmic being appears as a mystical abstraction; among tribesmen, it is simply a deified ancestor.

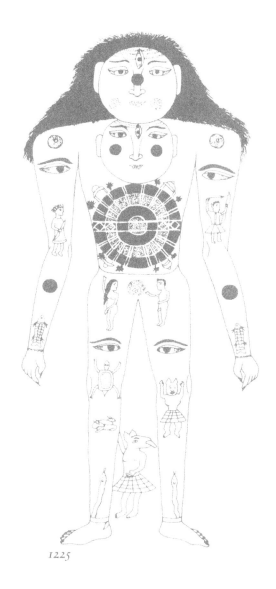

1225

Dismemberment

Creation of the human race from the *membra disjecta* of a prototypic human being implies human sacrifice. The allusion to such a sacrifice in the Vedic hymn of a sacrificial cosmic being seems merely allegorical, but reality probably preceded allegory. Presumably in pre-Vedic times, human beings were sacrificed, perhaps periodically, to symbolize the creation, or periodic re-creation of the world and of mankind.

A human sacrifice, symbolizing the Creation, is *ipso facto*, the archetypal sacrifice. If such rituals recapitulate Creation and the dismembered parts of the victim are associated with divisions of the social body which he symbolizes, is there a special disposition of the limbs?

Cannibal practices vary enormously, and it's difficult to disengage symbolic motives from savagery and eating habits. Still, we often find an emphasis upon arms & legs, or hands & feet, which may be due to something more than a gourmet's interest in a 'joint' of meat.

When Staden depicts four Tupinamba women racing around the huts of their camp, each carrying one of the freshly dismembered limbs of the victim, *1226*, this may be more than an expression of cannibal joy pure & simple. I believe this association of the four 'quarters' of the victim with the four geographical & social quarters of the camp symbolizes that the sacrifice recreates the Tupinamba world.

1226

A predilection for the arms & legs & feet of the victim as cannibal tidbits may stem ultimately from the recognition of the importance of these parts in terms of this same concept[121]. Aztec kings and Nicaro nobles reserved victims' thighs for consumption[122]. I doubt that this choice was dictated by purely epicurean considerations. Though its original motivation may have been forgotten, that choice was probably rooted in the same idea as the Tupinamba treatment of the four limbs.

Perhaps for this reason victim's arms & legs, hands & feet, even fingers & toes, were widely regarded as special cannibal delicacies or reserved as perquisites of chiefs & nobles.

Volhard cites evidence of this preference among tribes in southeast Australia, Papua, Loyalty Islands, New Caledonia, Fiji, Africa & Madagascar[123]. He cites, as well, two African instances of an *avoidance* of eating the tips of the fingers & toes in cases where the victim had been diseased, on the grounds that the disease was concentrated after death in these extremities[124]. Perhaps this idea—that disease concentrates in finger-tips—rationalizes the myth that offspring bud from limbs and that a special *potency* attaches to the fingers: a potency so great it could harm, rather than strengthen, the eater. I suspect the same motivation for the Kwakiutl avoidance of eating hands & feet[125].

1226

Among the Tupinamba, the victim's finger-tips were assigned as a special treat to distinguished guests[126]. This takes on significance in the light of an episode in a creation myth of the Bacairí according to which 'the first woman' (who was herself subsequently killed, dismembered & eaten), became pregnant by swallowing the finger-bones of dead Bacairí Indians.

The Guarani (southern Tupi) cut off the right thumb of the sacrificial victim before dismembering his body for the cooking pot[127]. Underlying this abstention from finger-eating is probably fear of the great potency of fingers. The Guarani say this amputation prevents the victim's ghost from drawing a bow in vengeance. The real motivation, I suspect, has been forgotten.

My guess is that the Guarani amputation was undertaken in order to complete the 'killing' of the victim by inhibiting his procreative power: if the amputated right finger had been eaten, as among the Tupinamba & Bacairí, the object would have been to acquire, rather than merely destroy, the victim's potency. Thus the behavior differs, but the basic idea underlying that behavior remains the same.

In each case, if I am correct, a primary association of the fingers with relatives was extended to the *principle* of relationship, hence to the closely associated idea of procreation, and finally to that of potency (perhaps with the help of phallic illusion).

Potency of Fingers

The genetic potency of fingers comes to
light again in the Papuan story of the culture hero who was dismembered & eaten,
except for one finger: the next morning he
reappeared alive[128]. This seems to imply
that the survival of a single finger is suffi-
cient to assure the regeneration of the
whole body, in much the same way as a
plant may spring from a cutting.

Of the myths that are half-told, half-sung,
in Eskimo igloos & tents from East Green-
land to Siberia, none is more important
than the myth of Sedna. Sedna is variously
a daughter, orphan or mother sacrificed to
save the community. In this sacrifice, her
first, second & third finger-joints are cut
off. These fall into the sea to become the
seal, walrus & whale upon whom the
Eskimo depend for survival. Sedna con-
trols these sea mammals, and thus holds
the power of life & death over the living.
Since these animals derive from her,
hunting them is a holy occupation; eating
them is a communion, tantamount to
eating the First One.

Finger-mutilation

The idea that special potency resides in fingers is merely a specialization of the genetic role of limbs. But it may have been the other way around: perhaps social significance was first imputed to fingers, and only later were limbs conceived as symbols of social organization *&* relationship.

The reason for this inference lies in the custom of finger-mutilation–specifically, the amputation of one or more phalanges of a living person. Many tribes practice this custom[129]. Its practitioners offer various explanations, the most common being sorrow for the death of a close relative, or an attempt to preserve the life of a sick or dying person. The basic notion seems to be: 'For each joint, a relative; for the death of each relative, a joint'.

In other words, fingers are so closely associated with relatives that they become identified with them and are therefore sacrificed for them. This sacrifice is, as it were, a partial death of the individual, by which he partakes in the death of a close relative.

1227

The practice survives. Gardner & Heider illustrate & describe finger-mutilation among the Dani of New Guinea: 'One man, a specialist of sorts has further funeral duties. He is the surgeon-magician whose appointment with the little girls chosen to sacrifice a finger falls at dawn on the morning after the cremation. The girls come into the family house with their mothers and a few older male relatives. The finger to be lost is tied between the second and third joint, and the child's elbow is rapped with a hard stick to deaden the nerves in part of her hand. With a small transverse stone adze, like that with which a woman might sharpen her digging stick, the amputator takes off the finger, extended on a board, up to the second joint. The severed member is burned in the dying embers of the funeral fire, and the wound is dressed with a mixture of clay and ashes. The child may cry or not, depending on its age and temperament. Each knows that what has happened had to happen, and that it will happen again. When they were infants their own mothers had held them and played with them using hands that were mostly thumbs.

'Immediately after the amputation, the girl's hand is bound tightly with banana leaves and banana husk strings all the way to the elbow [1227]. With a palmful of grass beneath the bandaged elbow to catch the blood, the child will hold up her proud green fist for the rest of the day'[130].

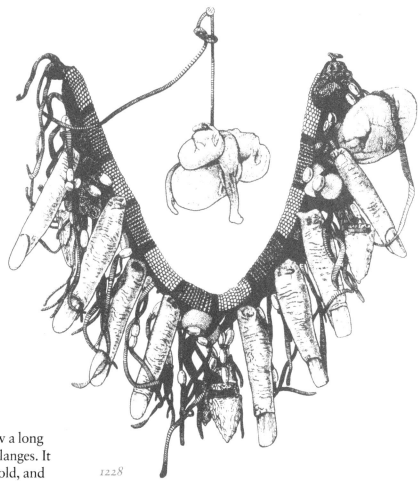

1228

In 1969, in southern Papua, I saw a long necklace composed of finger phalanges. It was intended to be worn, I was told, and though it wasn't in use at the time, it showed much wear.

Trophies composed of human fingers occurred among a number of American Indian tribes. Example 1228 was one of two removed from a Cheyenne village destroyed by cavalry in 1876. It was said to consist of left-hand, middle fingers of Indians of hostile tribes, killed by High Wolf, a Cheyenne warrior. Bourke, who published this example, cited a wide range of examples from other parts of the world[131].

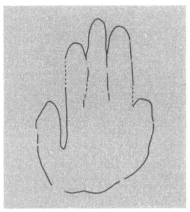

1229

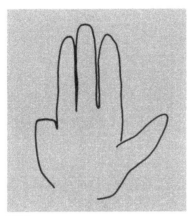

1230

A custom occurring so widely suggests an ancient origin. And we have evidence of its antiquity. Silhouettes of hands with missing fingers or parts of fingers, eg *1229–1231*, were projected on cave walls in southern France and northern Spain in the Aurignacian period, some 20,000 years ago[132]. Similar motifs occur on rock-paintings in Texas, *1232*, and in caves of southern Patagonia, *1233–1235*. New World examples remain undated, perhaps undatable, but I think the custom of finger-mutilation reached both Americas long ago[133].

Those who practice this custom generally say they mourn close relatives. If this motive also prevailed in ancient times, then it follows that fingers may have been conceived, already some 20,000 years ago, as representing relatives or degrees of relationship.

1231

1233

1232

1234

1235

Fingers & Digits

Associating relatives with finger-joints presumably arose through the use of fingers as digits in counting relatives for purposes of social classification. I assume this numerative function led, at very early times, to the actual identification of fingers with particular relatives or classes of relatives.

Among peoples with limited interest in numerary abstraction, counting may have taken place first on the fingers as units. But probably from early times the counting was done on knuckles or phalanges, as some Australian aborigines counted until recently[134]. Degrees of relationship were probably symbolized progressively from the distal to the proximal joint of each finger.

We don't know, of course, precisely what relationships were assigned to various parts of the fingers in Aurignacian times. Presumably modes of counting varied from one people to another. Since it is impossible to amputate the second or third phalanx of a finger without amputating also the tip, the choice of phalanx to be amputated probably was not always strictly determined by the classificatory position of the mourned relative on the hand, but reflected only a generalized association between relatives & fingers.

Nevertheless, the best explanation for this custom of amputating fingers as a sign of mourning for deceased relatives begins by assuming that the fingers were first used for classifying relatives, and then were identified with them.

Hand-prints

The hand-print has been popular in tribal art from very early times. Among recent tribesmen, it was often painted or stamped directly on the human body.

In Patagonia, Tehuelche men, at festivals & dances, used white paint, or powdered gypsum moistened & rubbed in the hand, to make five white finger-marks over their chests, arms & legs[135]. Among the Mohave, both sexes drew designs with wet, white paint on the palm of the hand, then pressed or stamped these designs repeatedly over the body or hair[136]. In 1907, a Pima Indian in California, *1236*, was marked with hand-prints of powdered soap-stone, in preparation for a curing rite.

Ahlbrinck, after describing delicate, intricate patterns painted by the Waiana Indians of Guiana upon their bodies, observes: 'A decoration which all Waiana women (but not the men) applied to themselves I find less beautiful, and in fact ugly. When the painting [of intricate patterns] is finished, they slap the open hand with widely separated fingers on their bodies, front and back, making black impressions of the palm and fingers, which stand out in wild and freakish contrast to the well-ordered designs'[137].

1236

1237

1238

1239

232

The painted, or more probably impressed, image of a hand upon the left breast of a Mandan chief, *1237*, was said to indicate he had taken captives. A contemporary description, as well as the illustration itself, suggest that a hand was dipped in yellow pigment, then stamped *over* a pattern of alternately brown *&* unpigmented stripes covering the whole upper body, thus creating a silhouette effect.

In the same way, a number of yellow bars, said to represent a tally of brave deeds, were drawn by the fingers (*nota bene!*) across the brown striping on the arms[138].

If the hand is essentially a social symbol, by virtue of the function of the fingers in counting relationships (and perhaps the resemblance of outstretched fingers to genealogical 'branching'), then its association with an hourglass on the sternum of the Sioux warrior in *232* becomes clear: the hand appears as a numerary adjunct or tally of the human figure represented by the hourglass.

In other words, the hand, because of its fingers, has the value of a multiplication mark: it suggests the multiplicity of the associated human figure, in the sense of an impressive ancestry.

Among Plains Indians, few body-decorations were more important than the human hand-motif, painted or tattooed on the chest, eg *1237–1239 & 232*.

1240

Stylized hands, tattooed or painted on male chests, were common among Plains Indians, both in ceremonies and as regular marks of ancestry, eg *1240*. Tattooing merely made permanent the stamped impression of an actual hand. The custom was extended to clothing as well: *1241*, a Plains Indian skin-jacket; and *1242*, an Iglulik Eskimo shaman's coat.

1241

1242

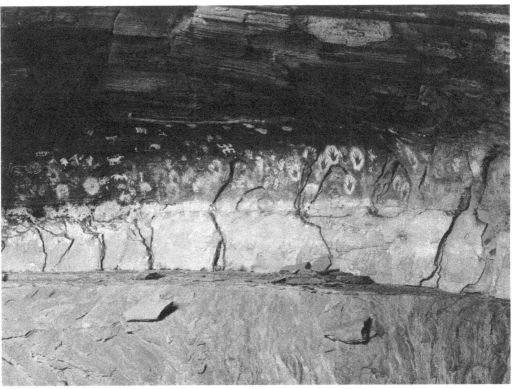

1243

Hand-silhouettes in Canyon de Chelly, Arizona, *1243*, have Old-World Aurignacian antecedents. A similar 'air-brush' technique of splattering paint from the mouth was employed in Patagonia, Oceania & elsewhere to produce 'hand-negatives' on rock-facings, as well as on certain classes of Pueblo pottery. I assume all of these examples perpetuate an old tradition.

This custom of impressing hand-images on the human body enjoys such a wide modern distribution, I wonder if it doesn't survive from paleolithic times. Hand-silhouettes and imprints of pigmented hands on cave walls may represent a transfer of this decoration from body to stone surfaces—perhaps to commemorate the presence of the respective individuals at some ceremony held in or near the caves. Examples are common in both Old &

New Worlds, eg *1243*; as well as in Oceania, eg *1244*. In Australia, hand-images were painted on, and cut into, rock surfaces, eg *1053*, showing hand & vulva motifs commingled.

1244

1053

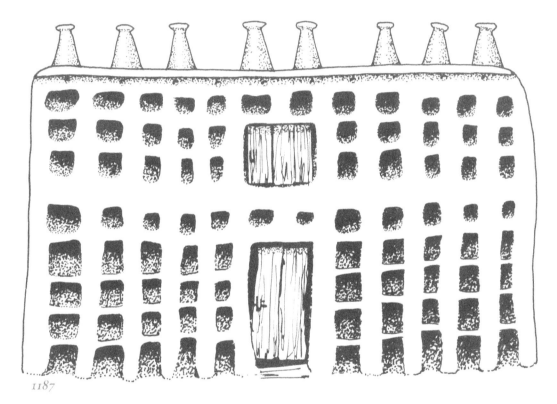

1187

The symbolism survives. The Dogon, in
describing the house facade in 1187,
likened it to a pair of hands spread out,
with the niches (representing ancestors) in
two series of five columns each[139].

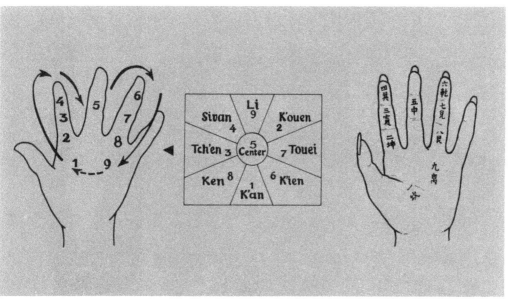

1245

In rural India today, one wall of a household is often covered with hand-prints, placed there after marriage and said to promote fertility. The Chinese practiced divination on the fingers, and used hands to foretell birth.

They also used the hand as a mnemonic device for the magic square: eight trigrams in circular pattern, with 5 in the center and the remaining numerals arranged so that any three in a straight line total 15, eg *1245*.

Each of these eight linear figures, collectively called *pa kua*, was composed of three parallel lines, either solid or broken in the center. A fortune-teller threw down, in succession, three pairs of yarrow sticks: pairs that crossed or touched counted as whole lines; pairs that fell separately counted as broken lines.

Three engraved pottery figurines, *1246a–c*, belonging to the Rumanian neolithic, date from about the middle of the 2nd millennium BC. It's only a guess, of course, that their body-decorations represent finger-applied designs, but such designs are so common among living tribesmen, I think this is a likely interpretation.

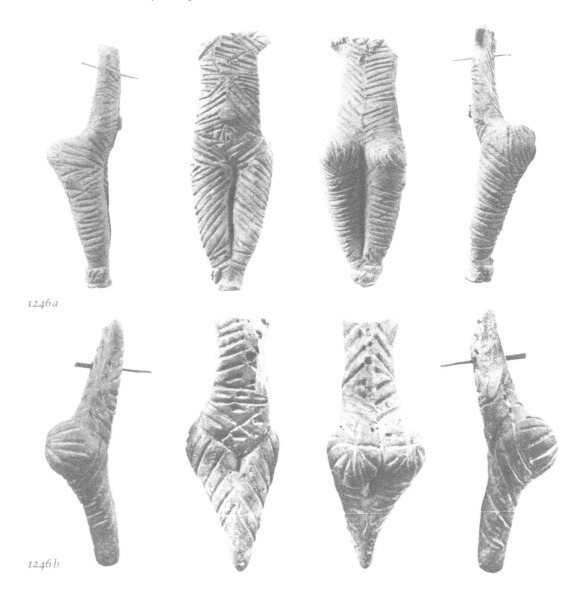

1246a

1246b

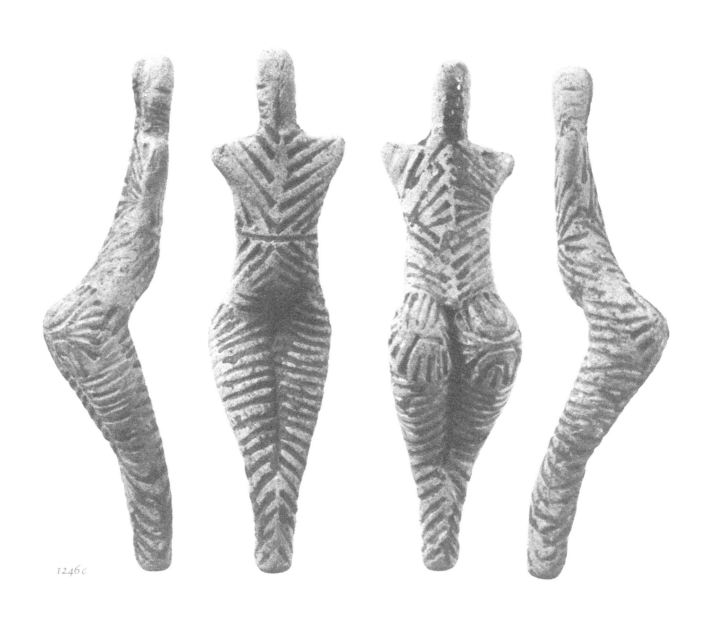

1246 c

1247

I suppose there is no simpler way to decorate the human body than by applying clay or paint directly with the hands & fingers. But the practicality of this method doesn't exclude a symbolic meaning. In fact, painted designs may be laboriously applied in imitation of this simple method, eg *1247*, Kikuyu dancers. This design occurs on a figurine from Venezuela, *1248*; on a stone monument in the Hoggar Mountains, Sahara, *1249*; and on a cave wall at Peche-Merle, France, *1250*. These last two interpretations might seem like the wildest over-speculation, save for the fact that the most common motifs on memorial posts and cave walls are genealogical 'emblems', commonly seen on bodies, robes & shields.

My thought is that most, perhaps all such examples, originally had genealogical significance. Sometimes this meaning survived, generally much eroded. But even when explicit meaning disappeared, traditional associations often remained, conferring special significance on hand & finger motifs.

1248

1249

1250

17 Joint-marks

1251

Human Body as Genealogical Chart

If relationship was first reckoned on the joints of the fingers and then extended to other joints of the body, this would help explain 'joint-marks', a tradition firmly established among so many peoples.

Human faces, skulls or eyes, symbolizing ancestors or relatives, are often painted or tattooed on human bodies, at the joints, according to descent or relationship. An individual, usually during an initiation, is 'clothed' in his tribal ancestry and thereby converted into a living genealogical chart, eg *1251*, a Marquesan male with faces tattooed on his shoulders & knees.

1252

▶

Polynesia

An Austral Islands 'goddess', *1252*, has a joint-mark on each shoulder, wrist, hip, knee & ankle.

▶

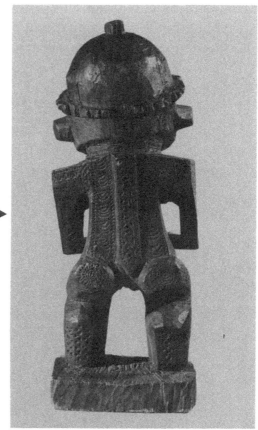

An Hawaiian carving of a human figure connecting two bowls, *1253*, has shell-inlaid eyes at the shoulders, elbows, wrists, hips, knees & ankles.

1253

▲

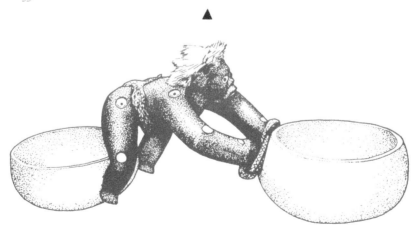

The eyes of the Maori carving in *1254* are inlaid with shell; similar inlays mark the shoulders, hips and one knee. These paired joint-eyes are really the eyes of highly conventionalized human heads, called *manaia*-heads: a complete human face is symbolized at each joint. Such joint-markings were a specialty of one tribe, the Ngati-Porou, who also produced *1255*, with joint-eyes at the shoulders & knees.

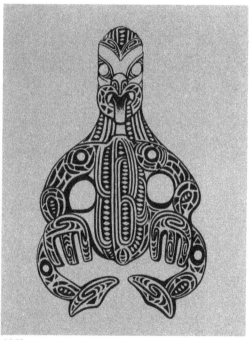

1254

1255

Melanesia

Of the many examples that could be
shown from New Guinea, I offer three:
1256, a Yuat River figure with joint-faces
on the shoulders & navel, and joint-eyes
on the knees; *1257*, an ancestral image
from southern West Irian with joint-eyes
(some even have eye-brows) at the ankles,
hips, wrists, elbows & shoulders; and
1258, a canoe-bailer from Tami Island,
with a ring on each wrist, shoulder, hip &
knee.

1256

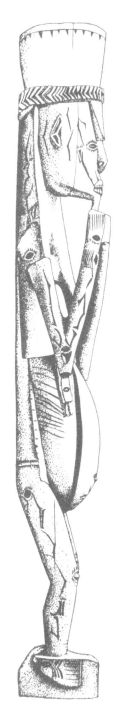

1257

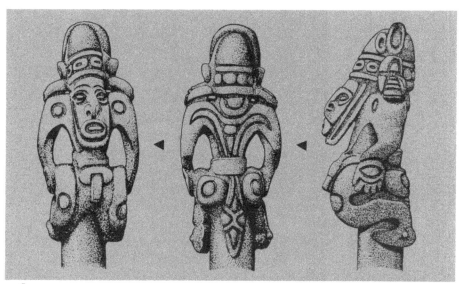

1258

A skull hangs from each elbow & knee of a
figure carved on a club from Milne Bay,
1259; while a memorial figure from the
New Hebrides, *1260*, has a face modeled
upon each shoulder & knee. These
'masks', we are told, represent certain
ranks attained by the head man. They may
be vestiges, in mortuary use, of joint-
marks originally placed on living bodies,
eg *1261*, a shoulder scarification common
in the Sepik River area in New Guinea;
and *1262*, another shoulder-scarification,
from the Torres Strait area, in the form of
joint-eyes.

1259

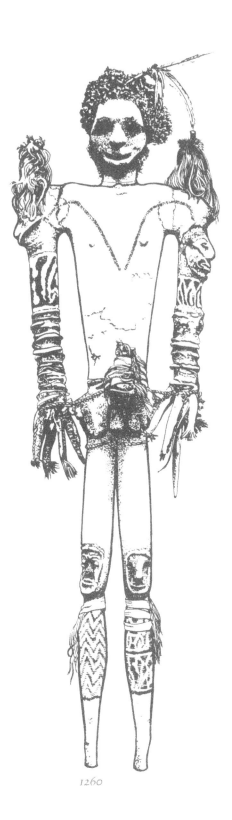

1260

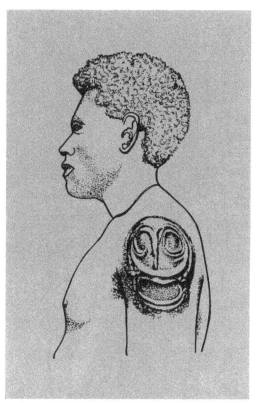

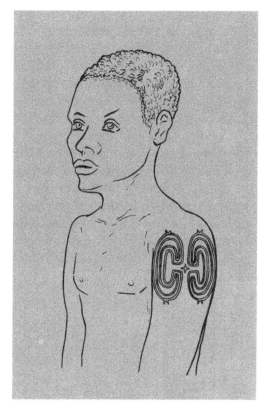

1261

1262

Indonesia & Asia

The Murung of Borneo say each person
has seven souls: one at the top of the head,
one in each eye & knee, and one in the
navel (the location of the seventh isn't
specified)[140]. Joints, then, were seen as
equivalents to eyes, and both were
regarded as seats of the soul or souls.

The figure in *1263*, with joint-eyes at the
shoulders, elbows & knees, and heads at
the shoulders, hips & navel, appears in a
Borneo drawing of a spirit-ship allegedly
manned by ancestors. A Kenyah sculpture,
1264, also from Borneo, has porcelain
inlays at the eyes, knees, hips, elbows,
shoulders & penis.

1264

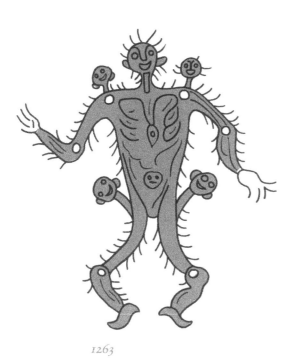

1263

Among the Kenyahs, in the greatest of
their Leppo Tau feasts, there are successive grades called *suhan*. Figure *1265*
shows a man taking 'the highest grade of
all', *taro*. Though he has only fifteen of the
long feathers of the Class B hat, that 'does
not matter'. He wears the skin of an
orangutan, an essential part of the top
regalia of the *suhan taro*. And, what is
most important of all, he has, as *suhan*
elements, eight human skulls: one under
each hip, ankle *&* knee, and one over each
elbow. 'The late Penghulu Besar of Long
Newang, whose house held the *Tree of
Life* . . . was the last man to reach *taro*'[141].

1265

1266

Tintiya, the Supreme Being in Balinese cosmology, *1266*, stands on the World Turtle, who is bound with a continuous rope so he will not cause earthquakes. We see Tintiya here in both benign *&* angry moods. Both examples have flame-like protrusions (hands?) at their major joints *&* genitals.

Whorl-like joint-marks on human figures appear in some of the earliest Sanskrit inscriptions in Java, eg *1267*. Similar motifs appeared on sculptures of mythic creatures in southeast Asia during the bronze age.

1267

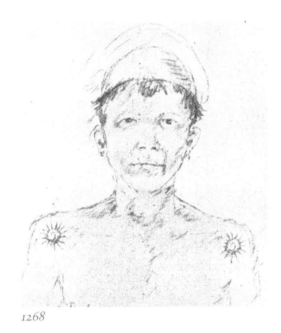

1268

Shoulder-markings on Kenyah men in Borneo, eg *1268*, may survive from this ancient custom of placing whorl-motifs on the joints, especially shoulder-joints, of deities and all who claim descent from them.

Tattooed shoulder rosettes weren't restricted to Java or Borneo. On San Cristoval Island in the southwest Solomons a rayed 'sun' was cut in the shoulders of youths upon admission to the chiefly clan[142]. On Rotuma, north of Fiji, rayed rosettes were tattooed on shoulders[143]. These were also a common, if not regular, feature of shoulder-tattooing in the Marquesas[144].

Both the shoulder-rosette & joint-whorl occur sporadically throughout other areas of Oceania and even more sporadically in Asia and the Mediterranean region. Among the Roman treasures found at Mildenhall, England, one silver plate, *1269*, shows a Gorgon figure with joint-whorls at its elbows & knees, and other figures with shoulder-whorls.

In European lore, there's the theme of the child lost by chance or treachery, then rediscovered. He's recognized by a royal cross, 'redder than the rose of summer', on his right shoulder. In medieval romances, those who discover this fateful mark, even before they can assign the predestined hero a precise genealogy, don't hesitate to exclaim, like the countess who rescues Richard le Beau, abandoned soon after birth in the forest: 'O God', said she, 'he shall be king!'[145].

1269

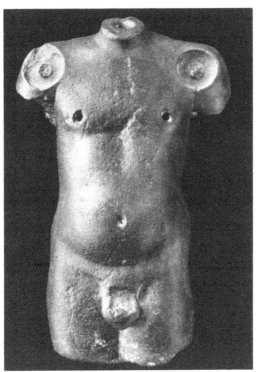

1270

A miniature, stone torso from India, 4th century BC, in pseudo-Greek style, *1270*, has a cavity in each front shoulder, presumably to hold a precious inlay. Such marks may have been painted or tattooed on ancient Indians[146].

A bronze figurine from Mongolia or North China, *1271*, has disks at the knees, shoulders, wrists and possibly the genitals. The terra cotta figurine in *1272*, from the Late Jomon culture of Japan, circa 2500–1000 BC, has markings at the shoulders, wrists, elbows, hips, knees & ankles. And a Shang dynasty stone figurine from Szu P'an Mo, China, *1273*, wears a robe decorated with eye-forms at the shoulders, hips and (lacking 'pupils') at the back of each shoulder. There is also a circle, with interior cross, at each ankle, and a horned animal's head at the genitals.

1273

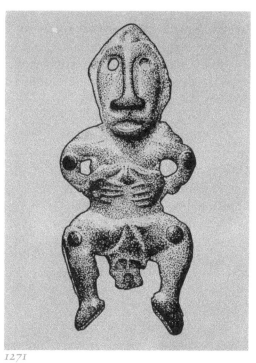

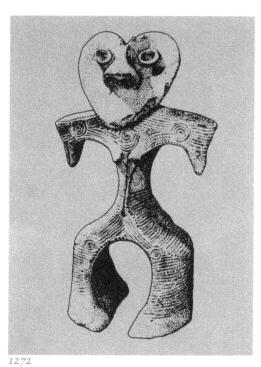

1271

1272

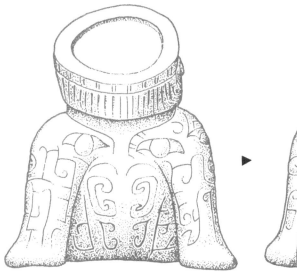

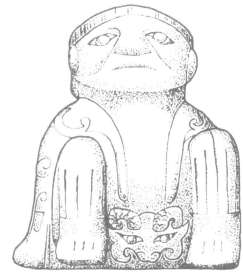

Siberia & North America

Among the maritime Chukchi of north-western Siberia, tattooed joint-marks serve as hunters' tallies and once served as tallies of homicides [147]. Similarly, Eskimo men of St. Lawrence Island in Bering Strait 'are tattooed in wrists, elbows, shoulder-joints, back of neck, hips, knees and ankles with one prick in commemoration of some event – killing a whale, polar bear, *mukluk* (bearded seal) or being a pallbearer' [148]. This single-dot tattoo may be a rudimentary eye-motif.

A prehistoric ivory figurine from Diomede Island, Bering Strait, *1274*, has a deep hole drilled into each shoulder, presumably for inserts, and a smaller hole drilled into each arm, on the upper part, rather high for elbow-marks. Carvings around each wrist suggest a heavy jacket; if so, incised lines on the chest may denote a coat design, rather than tattoos. The figure holds what resembles the fresh head of a walrus, with tusks & moustache in the mouth region.

As early as 1897 Boas recognized the special function of the eye as a joint-mark in Northwest Coast Indian art: 'An examination . . . will show that in most cases [the eye] is used to indicate a joint. Shoulders, elbows, hands, hips, knees, feet, the points of attachment of fins, tails and so forth, are always indicated by eyes' [149].

1274

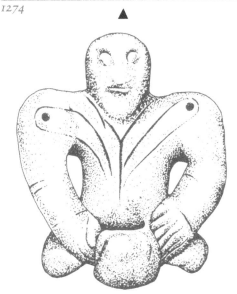

A bone container from British Columbia,
carved in the shape of a man, has
nucleated circles at the wrists, elbows,
ankles, knees & hips, *1275*. Insets of local
abalone accent the eyes, knees, ankles &
elbows of a raised human figure on an elk-
horn sacrificial club of traditional
Tsimshian form, *1276*.

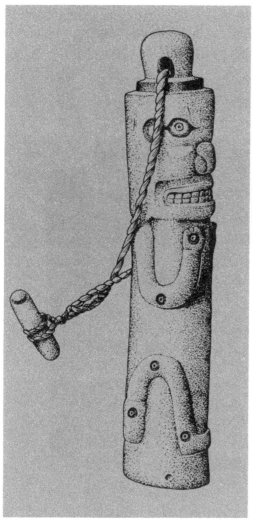

1275

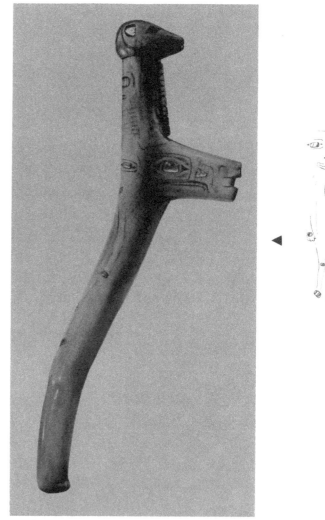

1276

1277

The creature in 1277, painted on a Haida
house-screen, has an eye-ring on each
hand and a ring accompanied by a tri-
angle (probably representing the canthus
of the eye) on each shoulder. A Tlingit
house-screen, 1278, shows faces at the
knees, elbows & wrists. Schurtz[150] suggests that the eye-motif in Northwest
Coast art is really the rudiments of a
complete face, and certainly the two are
often used interchangeably.

1278

1279

1280

273

In the pre-Christian Adena complex of the upper Mississippi valley, stone & clay tablets were incised or engraved in *bas relief* with the head, beak & talons of a raptorial bird with human features, including stylized hands & feet, eg 1279 & 1280. Note the simple dots and nucleated dots at the hip-shoulder, knee-elbow & wrist-ankle. Accumulated pigment in depressed areas of two of these tablets suggests their use in stamping, perhaps for stamping joint-marks on bodies or clothing[151].

A California pictograph, 273, has a disk within each bulging elbow & knee.

1281   *1282*

Two small gorgets from prehistoric
mounds in Alabama & Oklahoma, *1281*
& *1282*, are each engraved with a
mythical figure or costumed dancer.
Ocellations on *1281* look slightly mis-
placed, but presumably mark the
shoulders, elbows, wrists, hips, knees &
ankles. Nucleated ovals on the elbows of
1282 are identical with its eyes.

1283

Mexico

Joint-faces occur in ancient Mexico in at least two distinct cultural phases. The elaborately painted decoration of an anthropomorphic pottery vessel from the Huasteca culture of the gulf coast, *1283*, seems to imitate tattoos or body-paintings, including a face on each knee & shoulder, and at the genitals.

Joint-marks also occur in later Aztec art in the Central Mexican plateau, chiefly as an attribute of both the earth goddess, *1284*, and the mythic earth-toad, *1285 & 1286*. These were carved in flat relief on the bottom of stone sacrificial vessels and on the bottom of certain sculptures, especially those representing deities of Earth & Death[152].

The eyes at the wrists & ankles of *1285 & 1286* suggest hand-faces & foot-faces, with jaws formed from fingers & toes in the likeness of fangs. These faces, repeated at the elbows & knees, resemble snake-heads.

1284

1285

1286

1287

Mendiata, in the 16th century, reported that the Aztecs 'regarded the earth as a goddess and represented her as a ferocious frog, with bloody jaws at all the joints, saying that thus she devoured and swallowed everything'[153]. A 16th century French manuscript reads: '... The goddess of the earth, Tlaltecuhtli ... had eyes and mouths at every joint, with which she snapped like a savage beast'[154].

In *1287*, Tlaltecuhtli appears with faces on her knees, elbows, hands & feet; the glyph for 'jade' in her stomach; and an apron of skulls and crossed bones. She tilts her head back, her jaws agape to receive the dead, and at the same time discharges those reborn through her joints – a creation theme, for ancestors are dead and first-ancestors are tribal founders.

1288

Central & South America

Human figures incised on three Guiana war-clubs, *1288–1290*, show budding joints, some enclosing a dot; while the figure in *1291*, on a comb from Guiana, features disks at the shoulders, elbows, wrists, hips, navel & head.

1289

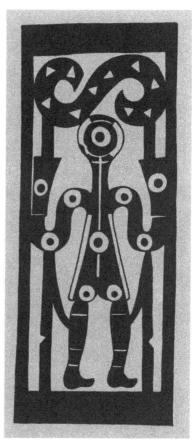

1290

1291

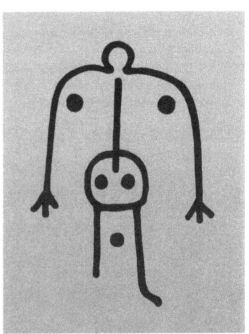

1292

1293

A Venezuelan petroglyph, *1292*, and a
Costa Rican figure, *1293*, display promi-
nent joint-marks; while various figurines
on pottery vessels from Venezuela and the
Caribbean, *1294–1297*, illustrate this
tradition less dramatically.

1294

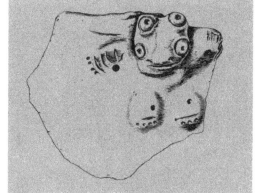

1295

1296

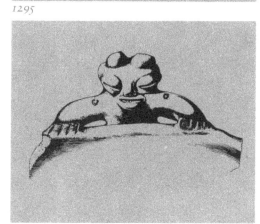

1297

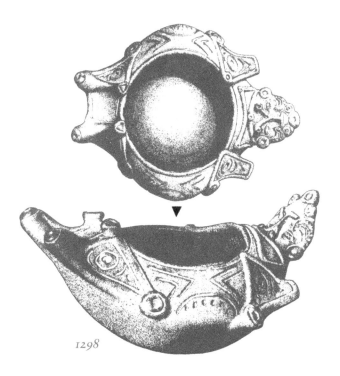

1298

A pottery vessel from Puerto Rico, *1298*, has joint-marks at the shoulders, elbows, wrists, hips, knees & ankles: a complete set.

Some Meso-American joint-marks are perforations, eg *1299*, from El Salvador; and *1300*, from Maracá, north of the Amazon delta. Perforations may prevent 'exploding' during firing, but their placement here conforms to other considerations.

Figure *1301* shows a wooden figurine from Santo Domingo, with ring-like ocellation on the hip & shoulder of the larger figure; an ovoid protuberance on its ankle, and an ocellation on the shoulder of the smaller figure on its back. The hip-ring may have held an inlay.

An anthropomorphic carving at the front of a ceremonial stool or *duho* from the Bahamas, *1302*, has each shoulder marked by a shallow, round depression with a raised rim. Such depressions were probably filled with 'stones, shells, or nuggets or gold'[155]. A similar *duho* in the British Museum has the eyes, as well as hollows on the shoulders, inlaid with identical plaques[156].

Monkey-like figures on a Panamanian pottery bowl, *1303*, derive from a classic genealogical pattern. Alternately upright & inverted figures share continuous limbs, linked leg-arm. Human faces, similar to those on the upright figures, mark the knees of the inverted figures.

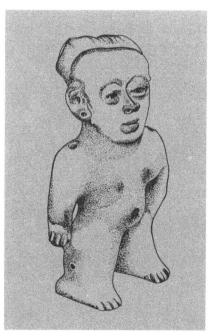

1299

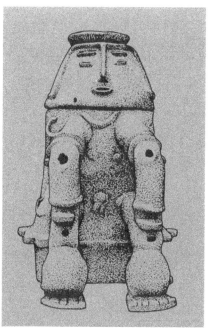

1300

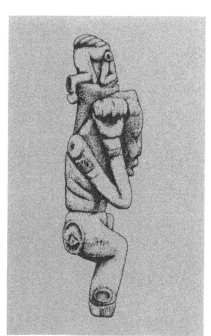

1301

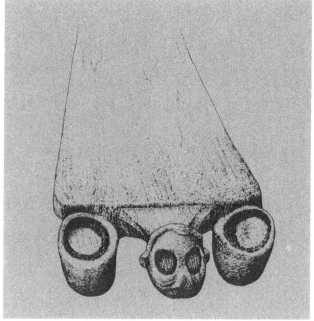

1302

1303

1304

1305

Complete, recognizable faces were
depicted on the joints of human figures in
several early phases of South American
art, including at Chavin [157], and Pucará [158].
Two polychrome vessels from Peru, *1304*
& 1305, have shoulder-faces & knee-faces.
So does a popular type of Nazca pot,
1306, which also has a face at the genitals.

1306

Vase *1307*, possibly from Paracás, has a
stylized second body, human or animal,
on the rear. Its main decoration, which I
assume represents body-painting or
tattooing or clothing imitating one of

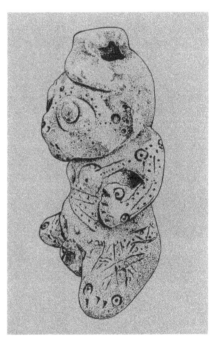

1307   *1308*   *1309*

these, includes eye-motifs at the shoulders,
hips & knees. Do these eyes belong to
animals (pumas, birds, snakes?) applied to
the body so that their heads & eyes fall
where they do?

Vessel *1308*, from Santarém, Brazil, has
joint-eyes on the shoulders & knees; while
the pottery figurine in *1309*, from
Maracay in Venezuela, has two nucleated
circles (paired eyes?) stamped on each
shoulder, wrist & knee, as well as in the
genital region.

This massive stone figure, *1310*, from the
Andes, was probably made near Pucará
about the 1st century BC. Note the Puma
heads with serpentine bodies at each knee,
shoulder & elbow.

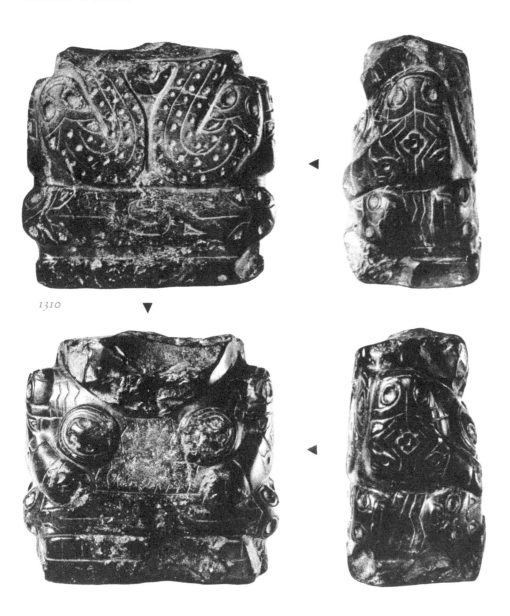

1310

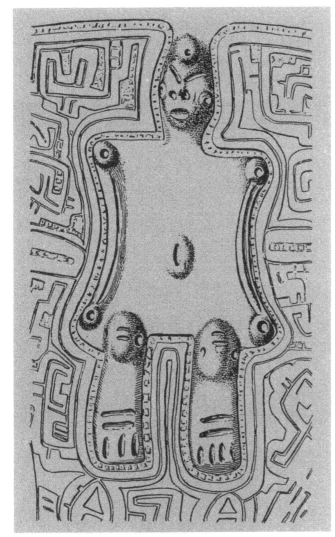

1311

Crater-like protuberances mark the shoulders & wrists of *1311*, a low-relief figure on a pottery vessel from Marajó Island at the mouth of the Amazon. Each knee carries two grooves across the patella and is punched at the sides with paired-holes.

In the decorative arts of this part of South America the same types of joint-marks found on human figures also occur on animal figures, especially reptilian creatures with flexed limbs. Thus a lizard on an urn from Marajó, *1312*, has shoulders, hips, elbows & knees marked by crater-like protuberances. And stamped-rings mark the hands & feet of two frogs which serve as opposing lugs on a Venezuelan bowl, *1313*.

In *1314*, a vessel from northeastern South America, two animals merge in one creature whose body coincides with the body of the vessel, and whose double-head and double-tail protrude at opposite sides. The shoulders, hips, elbows & knees are marked with eye-motifs.

1312

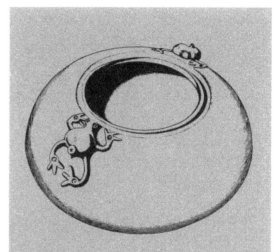

1313

1314

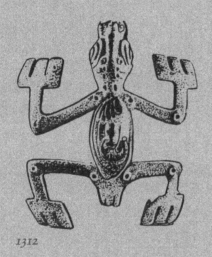

1312

1313

This arrangement of joint-marked frogs as
a confronting pair may be very ancient,
while the 'frog' or hocker motif itself is
probably even older. Compare *1312 &
1313* with *1315 & 1316*, the latter two
from Melanesia; then compare all four
with *1317*, on a neolithic potsherd from
Europe.

1315

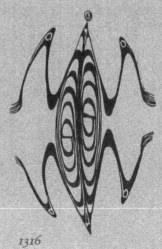

1316

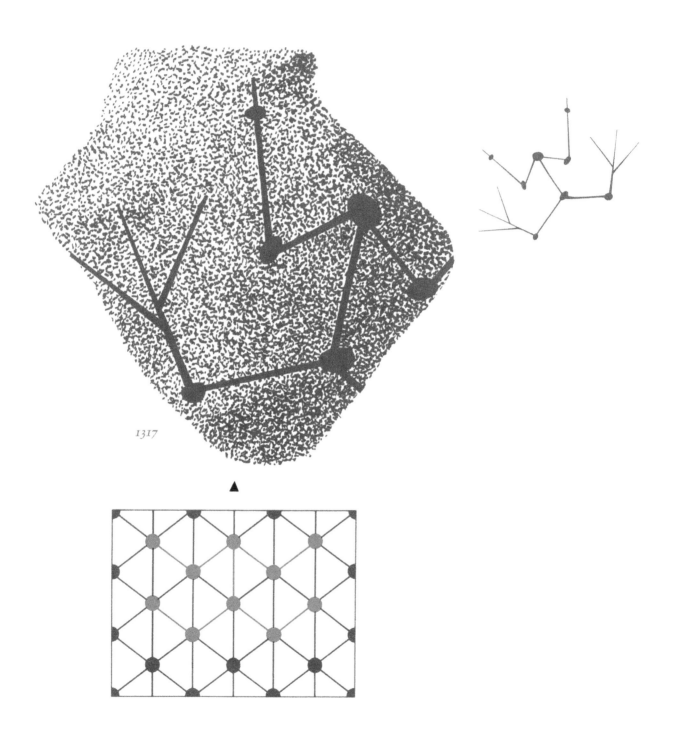

1317

1318

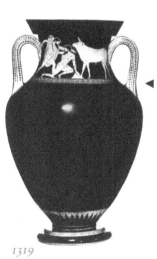

1319

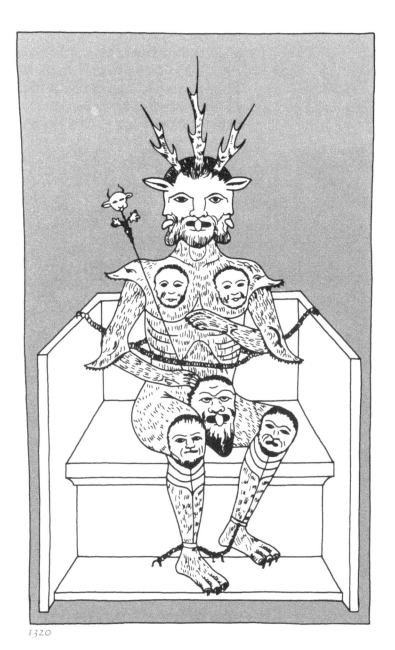

1320

Other Areas

In *1318 & 1319*, from classical Greece, we see Hermes in the act of killing the giant Argos, whose many eyes are distributed over his entire body. Argos was assigned by Hera to guard Io, whom the goddess had transformed into a cow.

A three-faced devil in a 15th century French miniature, *1320*, has joint-faces at its shoulders, knees & genitals. (In the United States, the penis is jocularly called a 'joint'—a euphemism of some antiquity.)

1321

Renaissance armor, especially that of kings, sometimes had faces at the joints, eg *1321*, with lionlike faces at the shoulders, elbows, wrists (also, knees & toes, not shown), as well as on the head and breast; or at the shoulders & elbows, eg *1322*; or at the shoulders & knees, eg *1323*. The intention presumably was apotropaic. This recalls the Chinese custom, popular during the T'ang dynasty (AD 618–913) of putting monster-masks, as protection from evil spirits, on the shoulders & navel of armor. Since the most common ailment of guards who slept on the ground was bursitis, these locations were appropriate to this rationale.

Renaissance armorers at times sought to re-create what they imagined was a Roman model. They were also subject to a variety of Asian influences. These two inspirations seem more likely sources for lionlike faces on armor than joint-marks, though joint-marks may have decorated Asian armor long ago.

Renaissance artists, seeking to re-create Classical traditions, may have drawn more heavily on local lore than they realized, eg the Fountain of Samson, in Fribourg, Switzerland, made by Hans Gieng in 1547: Samson's armor includes greaves with 'angel' faces at the knees and 'wild man' faces at the shoulders as epaulettes.

1322

1323

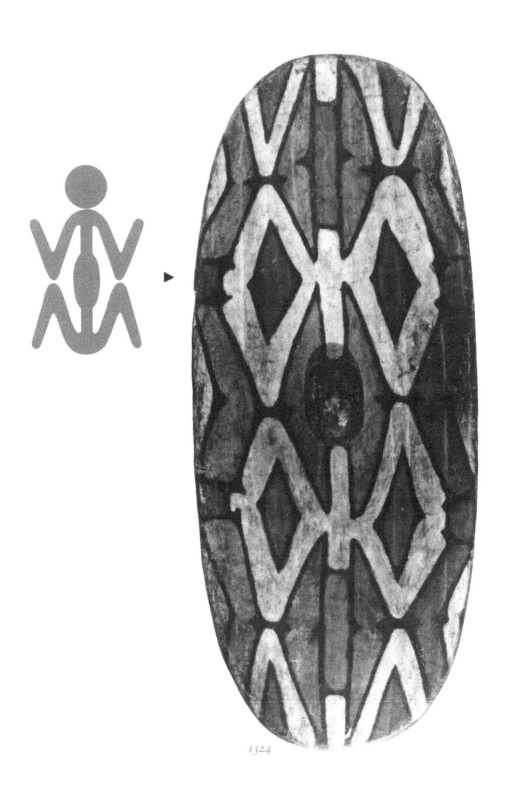

1324

Joint-marks are rare in Africa and unreported for southern Australia. Yet hockers are common on both continents, eg *1324*, a shield from eastern Australia; and *1325*, a Benin scabbard from West Africa.

Why this popularity of joint-marks in Oceania, Alaska & Meso-America; this rarity in Africa and absence in southern Australia? How & when did this tradition reach the New World? Has all ancient evidence perished, or are joint-marks merely a late by-product of genealogical patterns?

Joint-marks do occur among 'primitive' Papuans & Eskimos. As we've seen, certain paleolithic traditions survive in Papuan art. As we shall see, other paleolithic traditions survive in Eskimo art (cf 3:1). But Papuans & Eskimos aren't paleolithic peoples. Their arts preserve other traditions as well, including bronze age traditions, and it's not at all clear, at least to me, just when people first marked their joints with faces & eyes.

Australian aborigines who reckon genealogy on their finger-joints may preserve man's earliest method. Perhaps in neolithic times, conceivably first in Asia, genealogical reckoning by joints was transferred to the body as a whole. This might explain the absence of joint-marks in southern Australia and their rarity in Africa.

1325

1326   1327

Inter-arthral Disks

A curious motif of a squatting human figure, with a disk between each flexed elbow & knee, is found on several continents. Compare *1326*, a carved paddle from Borneo, with *1327*, a stela relief from Ecuador. And compare *1328*, a prehistoric Mimbres design from Arizona, with *1329*, a Dogon granary door from West Africa.

1328

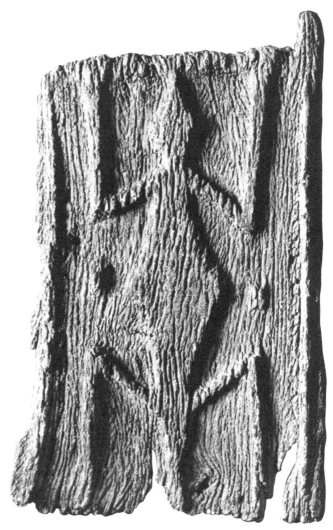

1329

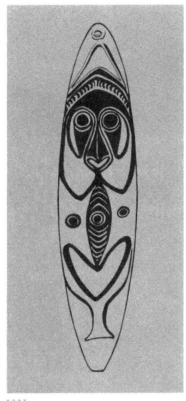

1330   1331   1332

Though executed in different local art styles, a shield from New Britain, *1330*; a *kwoi*-board from Papua, *1331*; and two paddles from the Solomon Islands, *1332 & 1333*; all conform to this general type. The same motif appears on two New Guinea carvings, *1334 & 1335*; as tattoos from Timor and Humboldt Bay, *1336 & 1337*; and in a New Caledonian petroglyph, *1338*.

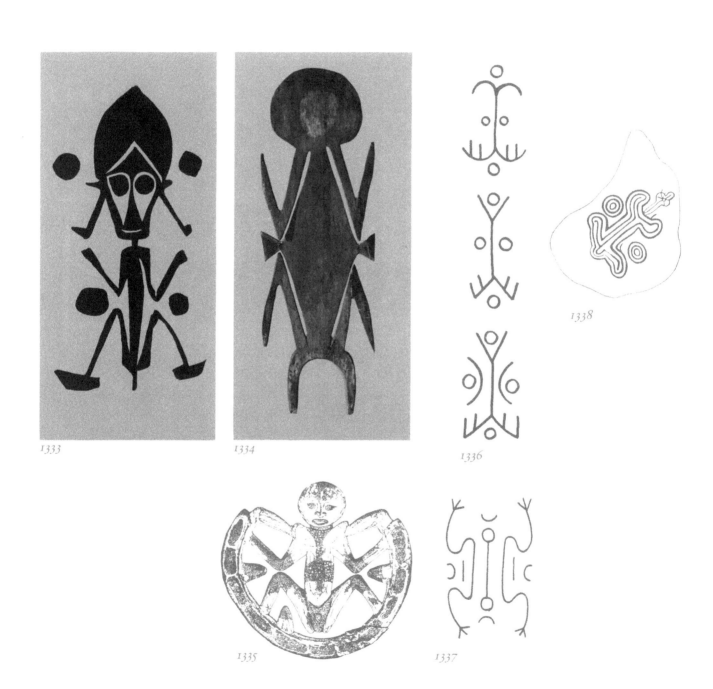

1333

1334

1336

1338

1335

1337

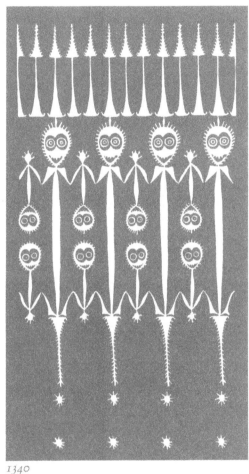

1339   *1340*

When such figures encircle a cylinder, they
share disks or extra skulls, eg *1339* &
1340, both Melanesian.

A Kenyah carving from Borneo, *1341*,
shows an anthropoid clinging to the face
of a monster whose eyes glower from
between the figure's elbows & knees. The
carving has the effect of a puzzle: the clue
lies in the simultaneous function of the
eyes & disks of the monster.

1341

Some figures are interchangeably men *&*
reptiles, eg *1342–1344*, pottery vessels
from Bolivia, Costa Rica *&* Venezuela;
and *1345–1350*, South American petroglyphs. Others are interchangeably men *&*
monkeys, eg *1351*, from Costa Rica.

1343

1342

1344

1345

1346

1347

1348

1349

1350

1351

1352

The stylized human figure in *1352*, from Argentina, has equally stylized disks. Some disks get debased, eg *1353*, incised on a club from Guiana. Some get transformed into local subjects: compare *1354 & 1355*, stelae from Ecuador. A favorite 'new' subject for disks was celestial bodies, eg *1356*, a petroglyph in New Mexico.

1353

1354

1355

1356

1332

1350

Some artists may have been unsure just where disks belonged: eg *1332* & *1350*. In *1346*, disks occupy positions appropriate for breasts, despite the penis; while in three gold plaques from Colombia, they appear between the elbows & knees, *1357*; under the arm-pits, *1358*; and as breasts, *1359*.

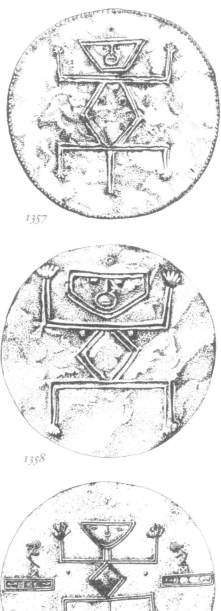

1357

1346

1358

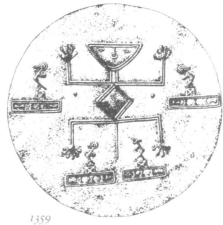

1359

A stylized human figure on an urn from
Marajó, Brazil, *1360*, has disks at its
shoulders *&* navel, plus identical disks
outside the body, or really between the
bodies, since this composition is repeated
around the body of the vessel.

1360

1361

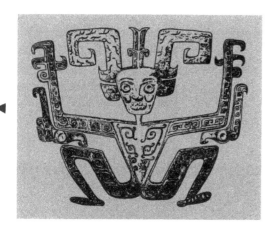

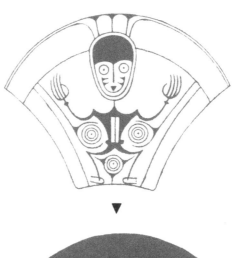

Despite such variations *&* vagaries, this motif is astonishingly consistent, considering its age *&* distribution. We recognize it on the famous Chinese Sumitomo drum, *1361*, of the Shang or early Chou period, circa 1300–900 BC. We see it again on a ceremonial bronze axe from Roti, in eastern Indonesia, *1362*, executed in a style reminiscent of Dongson art, which culminated in northern Indo-China about the beginning of the Christian era[159].

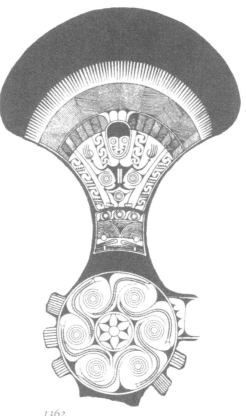

1362

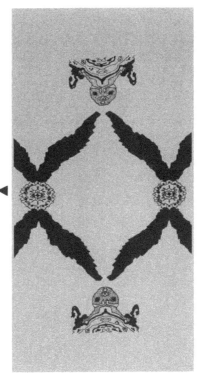

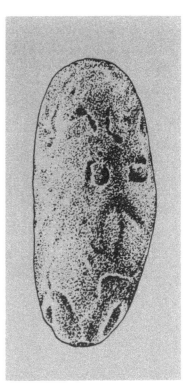

1363

1364

Inter-arthral disks appear on 16th & 17th century Persian carpets, eg 1363; and I believe we see them on 1364, an engraved pebble from paleolithic Asia. The modern artist who sketched 1364 interpreted this engraving as a human face and rendered the sketch accordingly. But the engraving actually resembles a hocker with inter-arthral disks, not a face. The time-gap between 1363 & 1364 is immense; so is the culture-gap.

76   1365

In sculpture, such disks fit neatly between the knees & elbows, eg 76, a head-rest from New Guinea. Elbow & knee marks may be combined, as in 1363 & 1364; or stacked; or horizontally positioned, as in 1365, a New Guinea hocker with joint-marks at the wrists, elbows, knees & ankles.

1366

I know of no better example of inter-arthral disks than *1366*: a hocker holds severed human heads by their hair.

This bent-corner box was discovered by fishermen, around 1978, in a dry cave near Sukwan, Alaska. Sukwan, a Haida village, borders Tlingit country: *1366* could be Haida or Tlingit, its style favoring the latter. Traces of red pigment remain on the body; human hair, secured by pegs, once hung over the tiny faces. I assume it was designed to hold a shaman's gear or perhaps a skull.

Evidence of weathering tells little about age in this fungus-rich environment. The age of *1366* must be judged by its style and that style suggests considerable antiquity. Its hocker-figures & merganser-heads are executed in early styles and the technique of repairing the accidental split in the front is also early: spruce root was drawn through drilled holes connected by grooves so that the root was protected from wear. I think this box is at least as early as the 18th century, but more to the point, I think its central motif is ancient in origin, classic in execution.

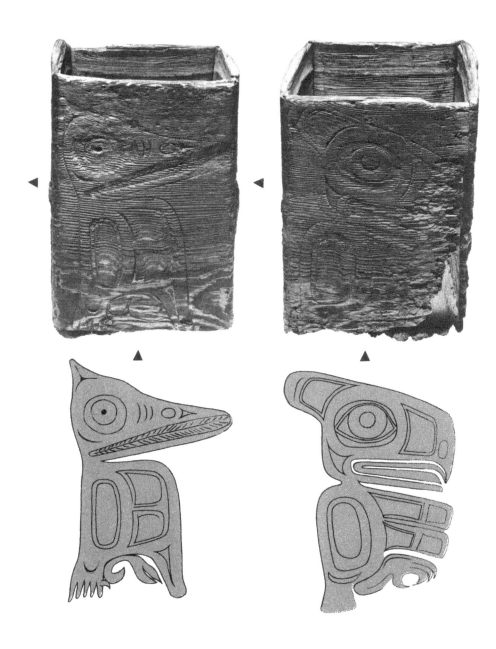

Similar disks appear in relief & filigree
carvings from New Guinea, eg *1367–1371*
and *147*.

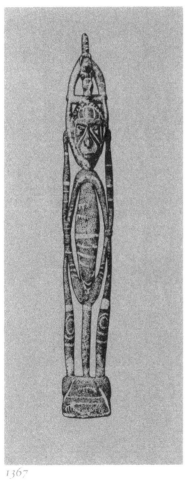

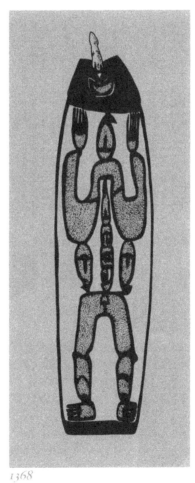

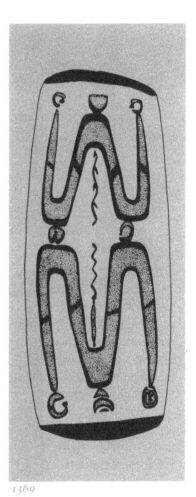

1367   *1368*   *1369*

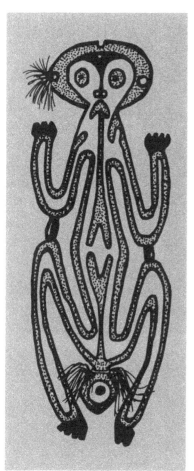

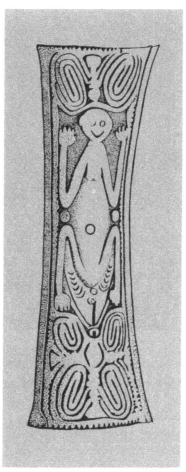

1370

1371

147

1372

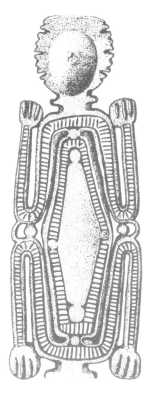

1373

Indonesian examples, eg *1372–1374*, are
often interchangeable with Melanesian
examples. And some Old World examples, eg *1337*, a Melanesian tattoo, are
virtually interchangeable with New World
examples, eg *1375*, a petroglyph in
Venezuela.

1374

1375

1337

Carvings of crouching human figures from
Indonesia, eg *1376–1379*, often have their
knees & elbows separated (or joined) by a
ball or spindle.

1376

1377

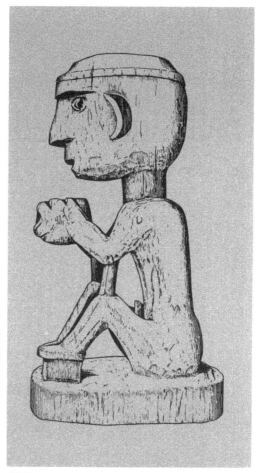

1378

1379

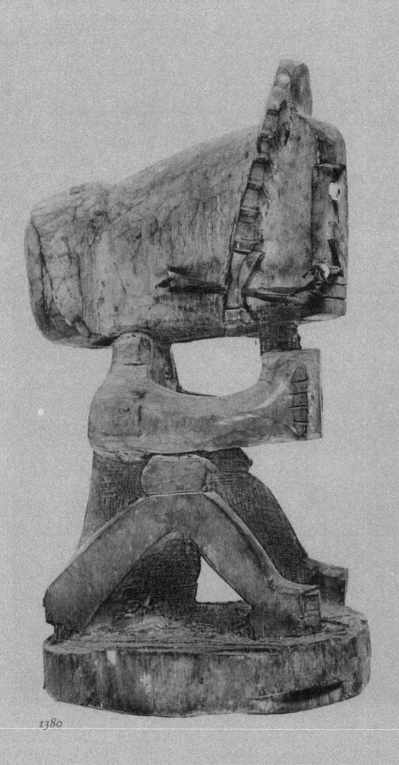

1380

Precisely the same feature occurs widely in
Melanesian sculpture, eg *1380–1382*.

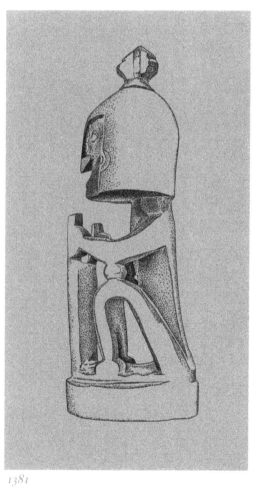

1381

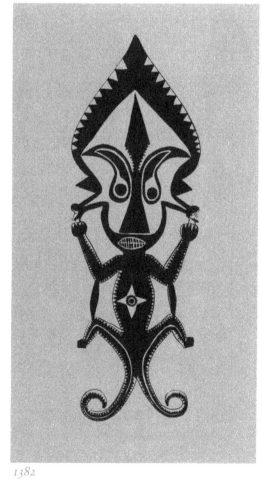

1382

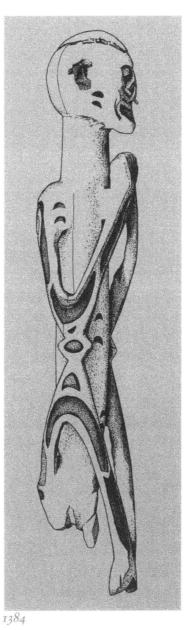

1383   1384   1385

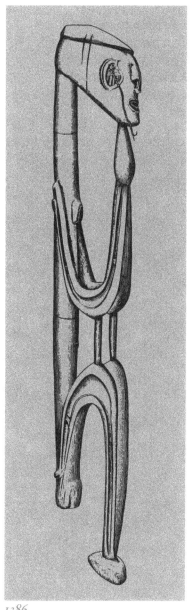

In each of these Melanesian examples, *1383–1387*, the knees & elbows are separated (or joined) by a ball or spindle or even something resembling a human eye, eg *1387*.

All these props lack anatomical justification. Their enigma yields best to one explanation: they express three-dimensionally the disks between the elbows & knees of two-dimensional hockers.

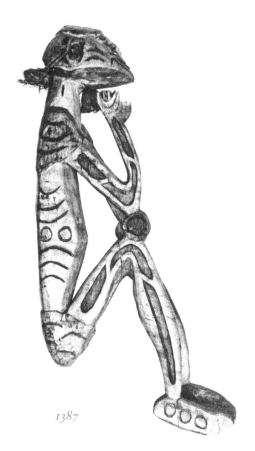

1386

1387

This is no local phenomenon. On the cover of *1388*, an urn from the Mosquito culture of eastern Colombia, sits a figure with props separating wrists from knees; while three figures from the Andean provinces of Venezuela, *1389–1391*, have ligatures between elbows *&* knees.

1388

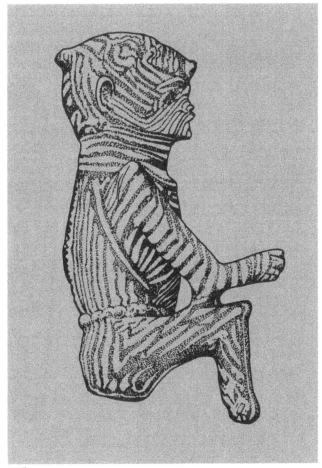

1389

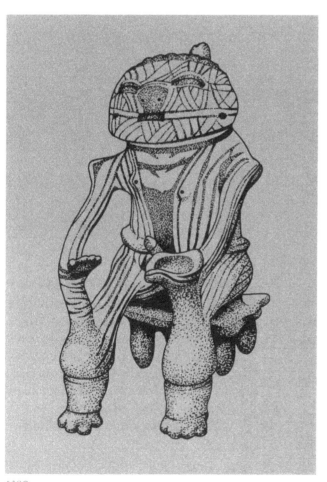

1390

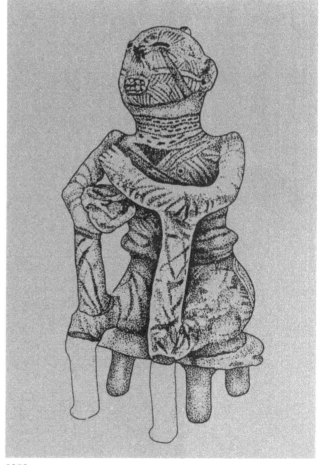

1391

1392

The design of *1392*, a bead-decorated drum in the Cameroon Grasslands, belongs ultimately with the design of the chief's chair in *1393*, from this same region.

Hockers with inter-arthral disks may find their explanation, at least in part, in *3*, a Melanesian club design. Here series of grinning, ghost-like figures with flexed arms & legs form continuous, undulating bands.

Heads in the intermediate tier aren't complete faces, but simply oval joint-eyes belonging to the figures immediately above & below them. Since the complete heads on the top & bottom tiers face each other, the pattern was clearly designed to be viewed in both directions. An eye, then, becomes a perfect symbol for a human head, seen equally well when inverted.

If we excerpt a single figure from *3*, what were once heads for lower figures become joint-eyes between the elbows & knees of the excerpted figure. A 'full' figure has, as well, joint-eyes at the wrists, ankles & genitals. So disembodied heads, excerpted incidentally when isolating a single figure, have no reason to be—unless converted into joint-marks or something else.

Is this the origin of joint-marks? I doubt if the matter is that simple. The whole idea of birth from limbs, and the widespread use of the human body as a kinship chart, obviously have a more solid foundation than mere mechanical mishap. But I think these technical problems were significant factors in the long history of joint-marks, especially in the origin of inter-arthral disks.

This interpretation would also explain why joint-marks often take the form of eyes; why they sometimes occur at the genitals; and why they are emphasized on the knees.

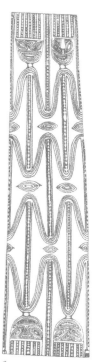

3

1393

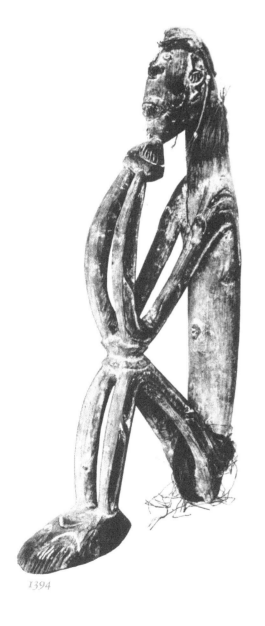

1394

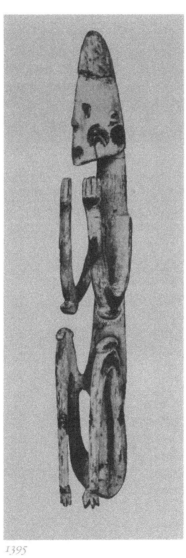

1395

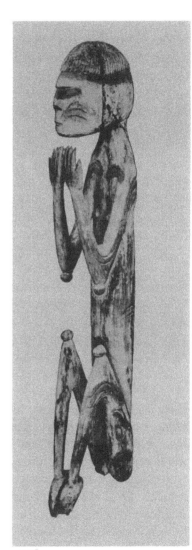

1396

What is important here is that all of these ideas about birth from limbs, genealogical patterns and joint-marks, largely support one another. Where they differ, both versions often co-exist. Thus, side-by-side with inter-arthral disks, we find separate joint-marks on elbows & knees, eg in New Guinea sculpture, *1394–1396*.

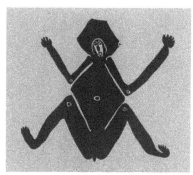

1397

This same splitting of inter-arthral disks also occurs on flat designs. Compare the hocker in *1397*, carved on a shield from New Guinea, with the hocker in *1398*, painted on a Mimbres vessel from Arizona. Hocker *1397* has joint-marks *on* its elbows & knees; hocker *1398* has joint-marks *adjoining* its elbows & knees.

1398

1399

A curious variation on this employs joint-marks resembling hands, sprouts or flames, eg *1399 & 1400*, from Irian Jaya; *1266*, Tintiya, Supreme Being in Balinese cosmography; and *1401*, Ma Chang vessels from China.

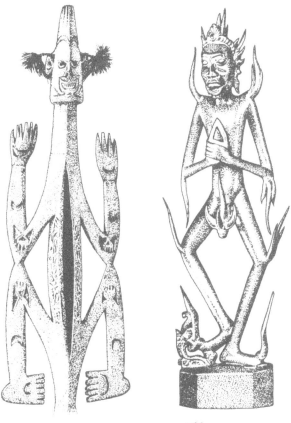

1400   *1266*

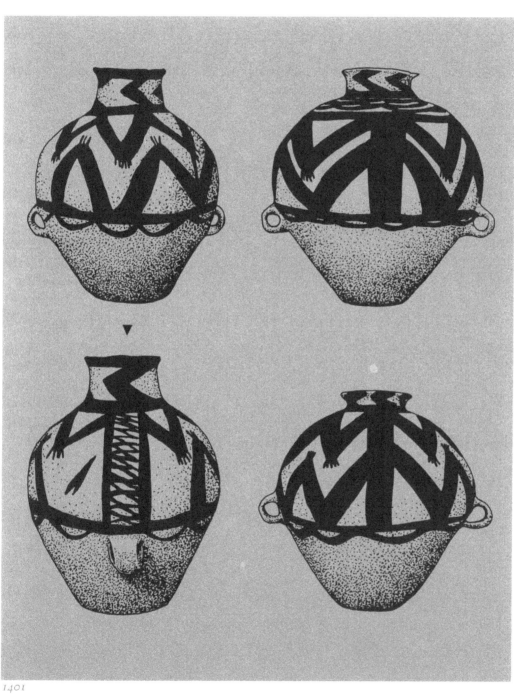

1402

When you excerpt a figure from a pattern of diagonally-linked figures, you sever its continuous limbs. Standing alone, the figure now violates the whole principle of genetic continuity which everywhere underlies genealogical patterns. More-over, that single figure no longer fits comfortably back into a pattern of linked figures: its bonds are cut. The human figures in *1402* & *1403*, on *ikats* from Borneo, retain now-meaningless disks and lack all meaningful continuity.

Such debasement seems to have occurred in much the same way in widely separated parts of the world, giving rise to similar forms, many of which came into being at roughly comparable times, often in areas far removed from one another. Various theories of diffusion have been offered to explain these remarkable parallels. The real connection, I think, lies much further back, ultimately in the early dispersals of peoples who shared certain genealogical patterns & beliefs.

1403

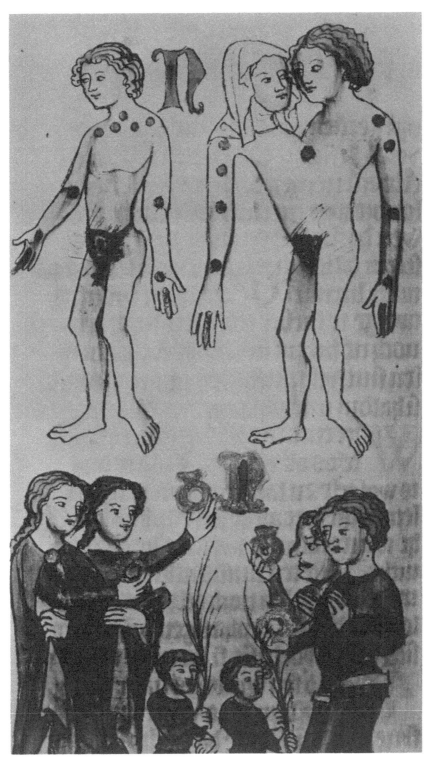

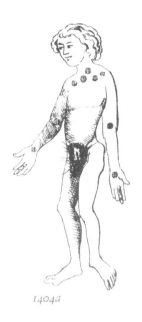

1404a

Medieval German Kinship Chart

The relation of joint-marks to kinship
reckoning comes to light in certain
medieval manuscripts called *Sachsen-*
spiegel used to record German legal codes.
Drawings such as *1404* illustrate the
sequence of relationship governing the
rights of inheritance: 'The father and
mother stand for the head, full brothers
and sisters in the neck, first cousins at the
shoulders, second, fifth and sixth cousins
at the joints of the fingers. Finally come the
nails, at which would stand the seventh
cousins . . .'[160].

Here remoteness of relationship increases
with the distance from the head, and
finger-joints therefore represent the
remotest relatives. Though this sequence
appears logical, it may invert the earliest
historical development: finger-joints may
first have been used to count relationship
and this count subsequently extended to
the joints of the major limbs.

Nevertheless, I doubt that medieval jurists
invented this kinship chart. I think they
simply codified an image from earlier
times. Among the Germans, at least, the
'primitive' idea of the whole body as a
chart of relationship is deeply imbedded in
linguistic usage. Grimm brought together
from various Germanic languages a series
of kinship terms, both specific *&* general,
derived from the names for head, nose,
cheek, bosom, stomach, lap or womb,
side, back, elbow, femur, knee, ankle *&*
nails[161]. Joints are included here on a par
with other features of the bodily
topography.

Obviously the body as a whole was conceived as a kinship chart, though only joints were specified in legal practice. The fact that *1404* makes no use of the joints of the lower limbs, which linguistic evidence shows to have been of at least equal importance with the upper limbs, suggests that the original symbolism was abbreviated here for practical purposes.

The single image of *1404* was invariably accompanied by another figure in which the human body, similarly marked at the joints, is surmounted by two heads: one male and one female. Examples from two other *Sachsenspiegel* are shown in *1405* & *1406*. Blood spurts, or plants sprout, from the joints & limbs of the two-headed figures in *1406*.

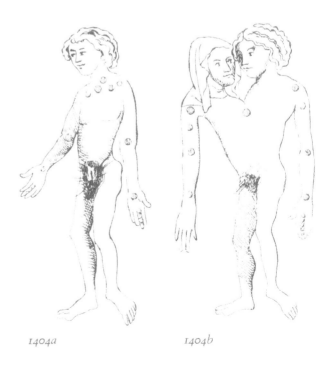

1404a   *1404b*

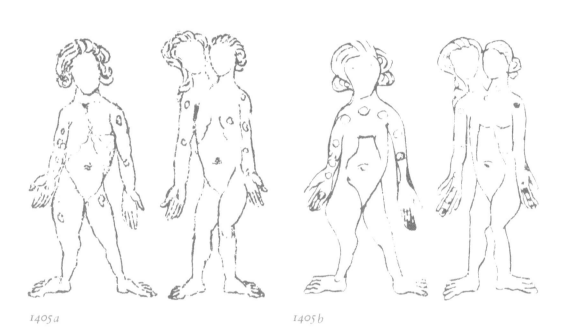

1405a   1405b

1406

This two-headed image ultimately relates
to the forked-post, widely diffused among
modern tribesmen and frequently both
anthropomorphic *& notched* (cf 2:1). I see
these notches as equivalent to the *spots*
inscribed at the joints of *1404* and to the
disks in medieval 'tables of relations', eg
1407–1409: each serves as a device for
enumerating generations.

1407

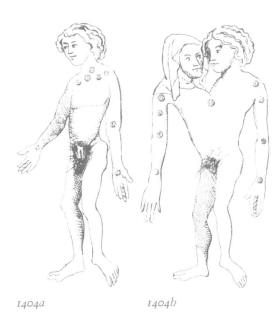

1404a   1404b

1408

In Teutonic customs, *wergild*—the indemnity required when one person killed another—was paid by the killer and his sib to the victim's sib. Theoretically, duties & claims extended as far as sixth cousins on both sides (ie to all of the joints, but not to the nails); practically, they extended only as far as fourth cousins. Rules fixed the total amount of *wergild*, as well as the share of each class of kinsfolk. The nearer the kin, the greater the sum.

This *wergild* was paid to those who possessed rights over the victim. These rights were held by the victim's cognatic relatives in a system similar to partnership: each relative held a share, and the share of any claim for indemnity depended on the nearness of the relation, eg second cousins claimed twice what third cousins claimed.

A man's kin were divided into those of the spear side (his paternal kin) and those of the spindle side (his mother's kin). In some Teutonic systems, relatives on the father's side paid or received twice as much as those on the mother's side, since a father's sister's son was judged a nearer relative than a mother's sister's son[162].

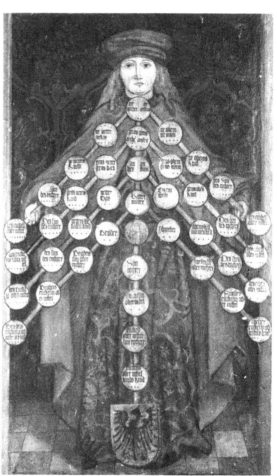

1409

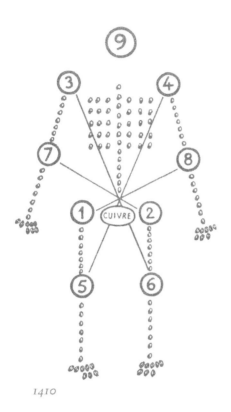

1410

Dogon Kinship Chart

The Dogon of West Africa lay out the scheme of a man on the ground with stones to illustrate the marital relationship of the ancestors of the eight clans composing their society. In *1410*, the four primary joints on each side of the body (shoulders, elbows, hips & knees) are marked by large stones, here numbered by the anthropologist for the convenience of the European reader to indicate the relative social rank assigned to them by the Dogon.

We are informed that the males & females of 'opposite' clans intermarry according to the lines connecting the joints diagonally across the center of the diagram. The ninth stone, marking the head of the figure, represents the chieftanship of each clan. The eight stones of the joints are explained as 'tokens of affection' left by the original ancestors of the respective clans, and as 'receptacles of their vital energy, which they wished to keep in circulation among their descendants'.

This diagram, which lives in the memories of Dogon elders versed in the lore of their tribe, was said to have been originally 'vomited' on the floor of a tomb in the place of the body of the first mortal by a primordial serpent who swallowed him after his death. The diagram is thus a symbol of regeneration, as well as a genealogical chart; and we are told that a similar chart, representing 'the human soul', is projected by the same serpent at every birth[163].

Both the *Sachsenspiegel* chart, *1404*,
and the Dogon chart, *1410*, symbolize
genealogy both by the major joints of the
body and by the finger-joints. In *1410*,
fingers *&* toes are represented by cowrie
shells said to symbolize nails. Joints or
finger-sections (numbered schematically
in *1411*) correspond to the eight major
joints of the body. Thus the fingers represent a system of marriage, each pair of
marital partners being coupled on two
adjoining sections of a finger (with the
exception of the last two fingers, which
'intermarry' with each other).

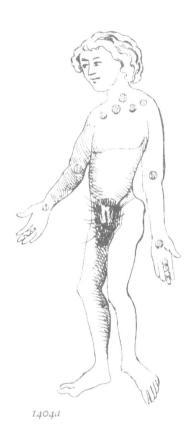

1404a

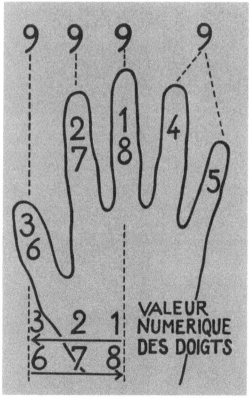

1411

Human Hand as Kinship Chart

The entire Dogon scheme clearly relates to the same basic idea as the *Sachsenspiegel* diagram. In both, finger-joints or phalanges are identified with particular relatives or classes of relatives and used in reckoning kinship.

In Taiwan *&* Borneo, human figures are tattooed on phalanges, *1412–1414*. The Haida of British Columbia sometimes tattooed mythic figures on lower phalanges, *1415 & 1416*. Eye-like grooves carved at the knuckles of *1417*, a Tlingit charm from Alaska, were explained as 'spirits emerging from the knuckles'.

1412

1413

1414

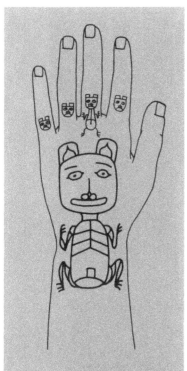

1415

1416

1417

An engraved shell from prehistoric Oklahoma, *1418*, shows a hand with an eye at
each joint; while two inlaid copper arms
from Peru, circa AD 1000–1100, *1419 &*
1420, represent hands tattooed with what
appear to be genealogical motifs.

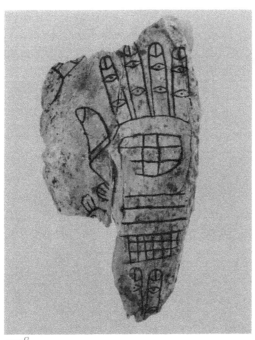

1418

1419

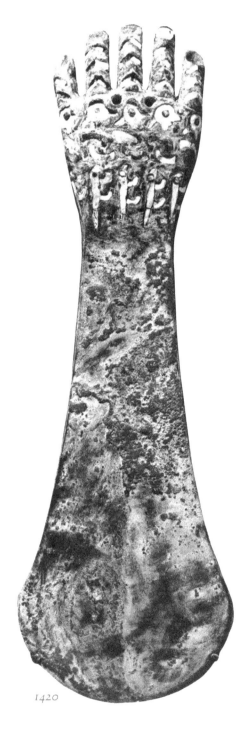

1420

The late 15th century German hand-chart in *1421*, with Christ & Mary on the thumb of an inner left hand, and the Twelve Apostles on the finger-joints, presumably served as a mnemonic device for reciting the Twelve Articles of the Christian Credo, shown at the right.

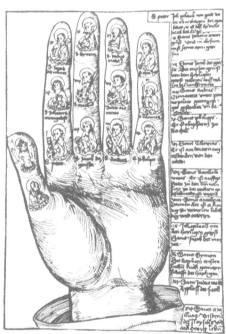

1421

Medieval hand-charts, with the intervals of the hexachordal scale marked on the finger-joints, served music students; hand-calendars helped pietists calculate the dates of movable feasts; and palmists assigned planets & constellations to finger-joints for cosmic divination. None of these mnemonic devices, as far as I know, related to genealogy, though the deities & intermediaries in *1421* are reminiscent of guardian ancestors.

Human Body as Kinship Chart

Joints merely connect bones; they disappear with the dissolution of the flesh, while the bones remain. I presume that joints were first conceived as symbolizing marital unions between 'members' of the social order, as represented by the bones.

Ultimate priority in the development of the genealogical concept may, logically, belong to the fingers, because of their natural suitability for numeration. But early man may have passed easily from counting relatives on fingers, to outright identification of fingers with relatives, as implied by the custom of amputating fingers in mourning. This identification could then have been extended to the larger members, and to other parts of the body. The Ammassalik Eskimo say that in every part of the human body (particularly in every joint, and especially in every finger-joint), there resides a little soul[164]. How natural to express this idea by using the human body as a kinship chart.

In 1950 I witnessed a dispute between two Eskimo groups, one Aivilik, the other Okomuit. When the spokesman for each group referred to kin, he touched the appropriate joint on his own body.

Lévy-Bruhl cites instances of counting in Australia & Papua which begin with the fingers on the left hand (taken as units, not by knuckles or phalanges), hence proceeding to the left wrist, elbow & shoulder, followed by the neck and sometimes features of the face or head, and continuing downward successively by the corresponding joints of the right side, to the fingers of the right hand[165].

Kaufmann reports a similar custom among peoples in the Middle Sepik area of New Guinea, including its use in kinship reckoning[166]. Similar examples are scattered through the literature. For example, certain native Australians count relationship upon their bodies, using not only joints, but other body features. Stanner writes:

'A number of tribes use signs to designate certain relatives. The usual method is to touch various parts of the body, each relative being represented by a different part. This is commonly done when silent communication is for some reason necessary, but often it simply accompanies the mention of a relative, much as many aborigines when counting on their fingers raise each finger to their lips as the numerals are ticked off. Doubtless the concept has a reflection in the belief that twitchings or strange sensations in parts of the body mean that certain relatives will soon appear. The Nangiomeri say that twitchings of the thigh mean that mother's brother is likely to appear or that something is happening to him. One informant from this tribe gave me the following list of bodily signs for relatives: right shin, brother; left shin, classificatory brother; groin, mother's brother and sister's son;

shoulder, father, father's mother; breast, sister's son; knee, father's father and son's son; buttocks or hips, mother's father; eye, wife's uncle. The lists vary between tribes'[167].

I don't know whether the Nangiomeri actually project their system in a diagram, like those of the Dogon or the Germans. Yet I see a psychological analogy between the Nangiomeri custom and the Dogon idea. The Dogon elder who communicated the image of *1410* to the European anthropologist was blind and thus unable to trace it on the ground. So he indicated the positions of the various ancestors and the social groups descended from them by tapping the corresponding parts of his own body. He did so exactly as Stanner saw the Nangiomeri do, and as a medieval German lawyer may have done when arguing a case of inheritance in court.

In each, kinship is designated by means of the human body.

The Nangiomeri designation of father's father and son's son by the knee has a certain parallel in the Philippines, where the Tagalog designate a great grandchild as 'grandchild of the knee'; and a great great grandchild as 'grandchild of the sole of the foot'. Fox adds that the Iloko-speaking people of the northwest coast of Luzon carried this system even further: 'Likening the generational position of ego to the waist, they define five generations by

the shoulders and head (ie ascending generations) and by the knees and the soles (ie descending generations). This is extremely interesting from the standpoint of social anthropology, for it bounds the bilateral kinship group as it exists in reality'[168].

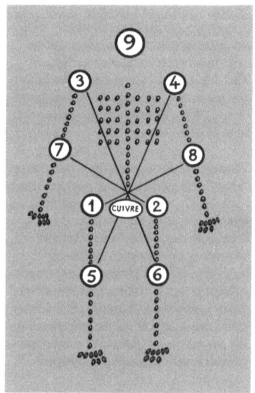

1410

Similarly among the Penan of Borneo, the term *tepun* for grandparent is qualified as *tepun lep* (*lep* = knee) to designate a great-grandparent; and as *tepun sikun* (*sikun* = elbow), to designate a great-great-grandparent[169].

The Yami of Botel Tobago tell the story of Vaoya, 'an ancestor born with a fish tail . . . at his birth the "grandfathers" of four generations give their comment on the unhappy event: a child with a fish tail! . . . The eldest says: I am the toes, the following generation is the knee, the next the breast. While telling, the man pointed at toes, knee and breast'[170].

Throughout large parts of Asia, the term 'bones' & 'flesh' designate relationships in the male & female lines, respectively, which determine the 'skeletal character of affinial nomenclature' (especially in systems of cross-cousin marriage)[171]. Similarly in Batak languages of Sumatra, *tulang*, which in ordinary Malay means 'bone', is used for 'agnate', while Malay *suku*, meaning 'leg', is the common term for a component quarter of a community, genealogically and often territorially[172].

The Mediterranean folk custom of threatening or insulting someone by clenching the right fist, while slapping the inner elbow with the left palm, signifies that one has the support of the kin group so designated. And both handshake and raised fist have remote connections with the notion that the hand as a whole signifies an extended kin-group.

Thus the structure of society may be indicated by the joints of a single figure (in a human kinship chart), as well as by the multiplicity of figures joined by common limbs (in a genealogical pattern). For the relation between individual & society is the relationship between microcosm & macrocosm: each is the image of the other.

In genealogical patterns, each individual appears as a member of society; but conversely, in kinship charts using the human body, society may be symbolized by the 'members' of each individual. The synthetic & analytic images of the social order are thus reconciled in the genetic symbolism of the limbs.

Animal Body as Kinship Chart

Joint-marks may be applied, in art, to hunted animals, thus creating a kinship chart analogous to charts applied to the human body. Hunting peoples often divide large carcasses according to that system, with certain joints or parts reserved for certain relatives. The hunter who makes the kill identifies with a specific part, which he may or may not eat, and the remaining joints go to relatives according to their 'relative' positions on the animal.

An Eskimo boy, after his first kill, formally distributes appropriate 'joints' to appropriate relatives. After that, the custom is followed without formality. Relatives who didn't participate in a hunt, who may not even be on good terms with the successful hunter, nevertheless can lay claim to 'their' portion—and I've seen them do so.

19 Human Sacrifice & Rebirth

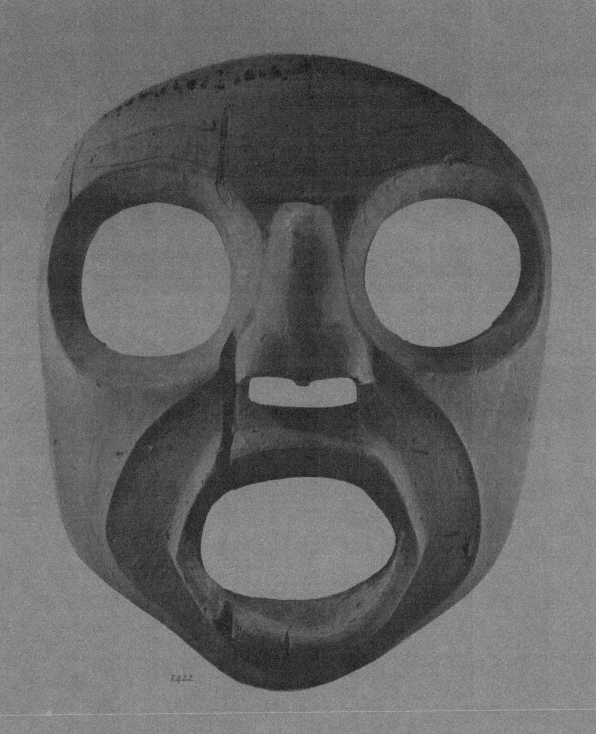

1422

Dis-membering & Re-membering

Earlier I suggested that the classification of
relatives probably first began on the
fingers or finger-joints and was later transferred to the body as a whole. Is there a
similar relation between finger-mutilation
and dismembering the human body to
symbolize the creation?

Such ideas appear to be related concep-
tually, but I do not know how they are
related historically. What is important
here is the co-existence of so many
mutually supportive ideas & practices:
identical kinship charts on the bodies of
men, animals & deities; rites of rebirth
involving passage through the successive
parts of a Primordial Ancestor; human
sacrifice & dismemberment; and myths of
re-creation involving the reassembly of
these parts or 'members'.

The Nangiomeri list includes bodily parts besides joints. This provides an ideal condition for the development of a myth of creation by dismemberment, analogous to the Dogon story of the primordial serpent. There a serpent with a human upper body enters the tomb of the first ancestor, swallows his body part by part, then creates him anew by spewing forth the swallowed parts in the same order, so as to form the diagram of *1410*, thus prefiguring a typical rite of initiation.

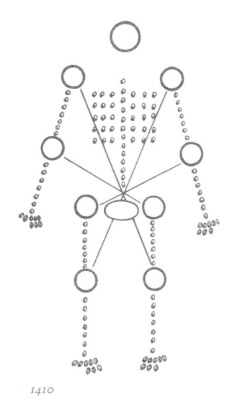

1410

I don't know whether the Nangiomeri or any other Australian tribe actually have such a creation myth; but other tribes of southeastern Australia observe a custom which may be regarded as prerequisite for such a myth. Thus Howitt describes the cannibalism practiced by the Dieri as part of a burial ceremony:

'When the body is lowered into the grave, an old man who is the nearest relative to the deceased present, cuts off all the fat adhering to the face, thighs, arms and stomach, and passes it around to be swallowed by the relatives. The order in which they partake of it is as follows: the mother eats of her children, and the children of their mother; a man eats of his sister's husband and of his brother's wife; mother's brothers, mother's sisters, sister's children, mother's parents, or daughter's children are also eaten of; but the father does not eat of his child nor the children of their sire. The relatives eat of the fat in order that they may no longer be sad'[173].

The parts of a deceased relative devoured by the Dieri may not agree precisely with the parts of the body associated with relatives by the Nangiomeri. But Dieri mourners partake of specific parts and identify themselves with the relative whom they eat. Assuming the deceased has 'gone to join his ancestors', and thus become one of them, eating the deceased was tantamount to eating the ancestor, and this rite was a re-enactment of the Creation by the dismemberment of a primordial human being, the ideal Ancestor of the tribe or race.

The communal eating of parts of a dead relative by the Dieri probably represents the survival of an immensely ancient custom which lies at the bottom of all myths of creation by dismemberment of an ultimate ancestor. Eating the dis-membered parts of a more immediate ancestor is essential to this rite.

Dzonokwa, the cannibal woman of Kwakiutl legend & ritual, is sometimes depicted in the form of aligned feast bowls representing her breasts, navel & knees, with the cover serving as her head, *1422*. Participants symbolically eat these parts of her body.

Substituting an image, or substituting a sacrificial captive, is probably a later development. In both, the intention of the 'endocannibalistic' rite is really defeated, insofar as the ancestor can be properly impersonated only by a dead relative. The importance of this inference will appear in a moment.

1422

The idea implicit in Dieri ritual canni-balism also underlies the many initiation ceremonies in which neophytes are ritually 'swallowed' by a mythic monster as a prelude to ritual rebirth. If Nangiomeri nomenclature is related to the familial cannibalism of the Dieri, then the bodily parts by which the Nangiomeri name their relatives presumably were conceived also as bodily parts of their ultimate ancestor. The Nangiomeri simply enumerate these parts. The Dieri eat them. And the Dogon have them eaten by a semi-human monster.

If the Dieri custom of eating parts of dead relatives symbolizes the creation of mankind, and if Tupinamba & Aztec customs of human sacrifice recapitulate that creation, we might expect to find some evidence of inner relation between the Australian & American customs.

In fact, there is such a relation; and it is so intimate that certain features of the American Indian custom are hardly to be explained except in the light of those of the Dieri. The specific prohibition of the Dieri against the father's eating of his child and the child's eating of his father has its close, if not precise, counterpart in the fact that after a captive of the Aztecs has been sacrificed, the man who captures him must abstain from eating him, *because of a simulated parental relationship*.

This is announced ritually at the moment of the capture, when the captor says to the captive: 'You are as my son', and the captive responds: 'You are the same as my father'. The captor may eat of the other sacrificed captives, but not of his own: 'for', he says, 'should I then eat of myself?'[174].

This correspondence with the Dieri custom can only mean that the basic motivation of Aztec (and Tupinamba) sacrifice is really ritual cannibalism, in which the parts of the body devoured are regarded as parts of a reincarnated an-cestor whose dismemberment is pre-requisite for the creation of the race and whose parts must be swallowed for its perpetuation. In short: each sacrifice, and more specifically each act of cannibalism, recapitulates the Creation.

The motive which deters the Aztec captor from eating his captive is the same as that which deters the Tupinamba executioner from eating of his victim; and the paternal solicitude shown by the Tupinamba for their prisoners (who often became the temporary sons-in-law of their captors) supports this interpretation. In Australia, relatives were ritually eaten when they died; in America, relatives by proxy were created for that purpose[175].

If the importance of the prohibition against cannibalism in the direct male line did not strike us in the Dieri custom, it is forced upon our attention by its conspicuous survival in a ritual like that of the Aztecs, which seems to be otherwise characterized by secondary elaboration. What is the significance of this prohibition? Why does the Aztec warrior justify his abstention from the flesh of his 'son' with the argument that this would be like eating of himself?

Apparently there is something special in the relationship between father & child which precludes their eating of each other. Why is this relationship different from all others enumerated in the account of the Dieri ritual?

Perhaps there is a clue in the naming of relatives by bodily parts among the Nangiomeri. Stanner gives only the list of parts which he encountered among one particular tribe, and tells us that these lists are variable. Still, I wonder if there isn't special significance in the fact that the Nangiomeri assign the 'father's father and son's son' just to the knees—since knees play such an important role in creation myths throughout the world.

In such myths, the ultimate ancestor from whose knees the first human beings were born is almost invariably a male, and in most instances we are given to understand that this birth takes place spontaneously, without the intervention of a female womb.

In other words, the first birth is exclusively in the male line. Evidently because of its exceptional character, the relation between all fathers & children is different from all other relationships, which are traced through the participation of females in the procreative act. This in itself might explain the prohibition against eating of the real son (and father) among the Dieri and of the fictive son among the Aztecs & Tupinamba.

Both Nangiomeri nomenclature and Dieri cannibalism imply the creation of a society by dismemberment: ideally the dismemberment of the ultimate ancestor, and ritually that of the individual who stands for him. Cannibalism may have developed out of, or in close relation to, this conception.

It's noteworthy that the motive of cannibalism persists in association with the Dogon diagram, insofar as the 'first man' represented in *1410* is eaten by a mythical half-human serpent. Among the Germans, at least in the immediate legal context of the *Sachenspiegel*, the theme of cannibalism has disappeared.

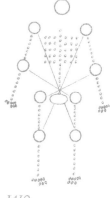

1410

Indonesia & Ryukyus

In Ambon and the surrounding Moluccas, designating social connections by parts of the body appears to be related to the communal eating of those parts in a ritual of re-creation. At least nineteen parts of the human body are used to designate not only individuals (as among the Nangiomeri), but also certain social groups, which in their totality comprise the community (*uli*), conceived as a human body. Even villages, occupied by clans named for the various bodily parts, are laid out in a geographical scheme simulating a gigantic human figure[176].

In this same region, ritual cannibalism persisted down to recent times and is still simulated, on certain occasions, by the ceremonial consumption of 'a glass of water as symbol of the blood, and various kinds of cakes representing the heart, liver, spleen, ribs, spinal cord (several Ambonese words for "spinal column" also mean "ancestor"), intestines, etc.' In ordinary sacrifices to the village spirit, each family offers the part (nowadays the part of a pig) corresponding to the place which it symbolically occupies in the communal 'body'[177].

Early Chinese records ascribe sacro-cannibalism to the southern Ryukyuans. Traditions of this still survive. The question, 'Do you attend the funeral?' is to this day rendered, 'Do you partake of man?' A death announcement was, until very recently, on Ishigaki, made in similar terms. Close kin are called 'flesh relations', distant kin 'fat relations', indicating the parts assigned to the respective assembled relatives for consumption. 'This consumption of parts of the corpse has been replaced with ritual partaking of animal's meat by all participants at the funeral . . . it was considered an act of filial piety to prevent the deceased's body from being defiled by animals'[178].

Similarly, in southwest Japan, the funeral feast is usually concluded by the words: 'Let's wash the bones!' Soup from the animal or fish-bones is then handed around. A variation on this funeral employs the term 'bone-rinsing'[179].

India & Europe

Human sacrifice emphasizing joints was used in rituals of regeneration in India. A 19th-century account of human sacrifice among Khnoistan tribesmen in eastern India states that participants take hair from the victim's head *&* saliva from his mouth to anoint their own heads; that his head *&* neck are introduced into the reft of a strong bamboo split in two, the ends of which are secured *&* held by the sacrificer; the presiding priest then breaks the victim's arm *&* leg *joints* with an axe; after which his flesh is stripped and 'each man, having secured a piece, carries the quivering and bloody morsel to his fields, and there buries it.

'When it is remembered with what care these victims are fed, fostered and cherished until the hour of sacrifice arrives, even at that supreme moment being regarded as something more than mortal, it will hardly surprise anyone to learn that, so far from being grateful to us for saving them from a cruel death, the majority appeared almost indifferent. . .'[180].

In France, in 1613, the assassin of Henri IV was torn to pieces by four horses in the Palais de l'Hotel de Ville. On the Isle of Man, in 1442, for striking any of Lord Stanley's men, the deemster gave this sentence: 'That they be drawn by wild horses, hanged and after that their heads were to be cut off, and set upon the castle, another quarter at Peel, a third at Ramsey and the fourth at Castletown'[181].

Generally the victim, sentenced to be drawn *&* quartered, was hanged by the neck, but cut down before dead; his entrails burned before his face; his head cut off; his body quartered. In 1814, fifteen Canadians, convicted of treason, suffered this fate[182].

Emblems of the Arma Christi, common from the mid-15th century, show Christ's dismembered *&* stigmatized hands *&* feet in the four quarters of the field. Medieval Christianity, like the Bible, contains many involuntary descriptions of ancient images *&* customs.

1423

Faces on Knees

The Tlingit Indians of Alaska, in various
art forms, place a face or eye at every
major joint of human figures, eg *1278*. But
on spirit figures (*yakes*), which guard
shaman's graves, they carve faces only on
the knees, eg *1423*–*1425*.

1278

1424   1425

This is also true in the Yuat area of New
Guinea: joint-marks are common, but on
large ceremonial figures generally con-
fined to the knees, *1426 & 1427*. When
authentic figures are sold to museums, as
sometimes happens, native owners often
first remove these faces: only scars from
this surgery remain. Figures made
specifically for sale lack knee-faces.

In initiation rites in the neighboring Yuat-
Marwat region, maskettes (*yekale-anape*)
are tied to the knees, and only to the knees,
of large ceremonial figures[183].

The early Peruvian textile in *1428* has
joint-eyes on the hands & feet, but full
faces on the knees and on a trophy or
ancestral skull. The chest figure retains
only knee-joints. This is also true of the
Peruvian figure in *1429*.

Note the knee-faces on the 'doll' in *1430*,
from Siberia.

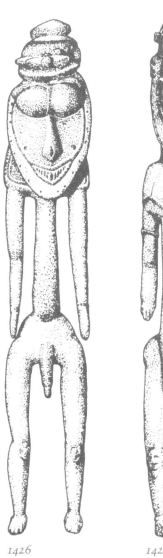

1426   *1427*

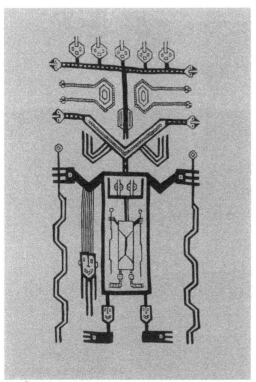

1428

1429

1430

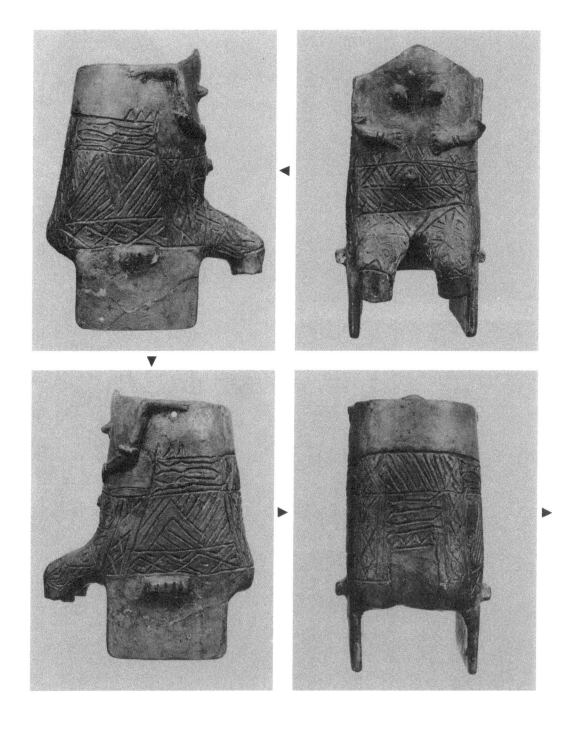

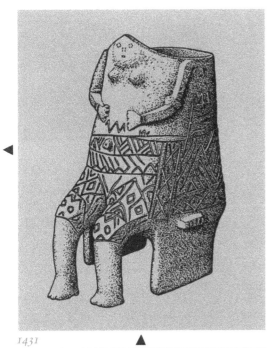

1431

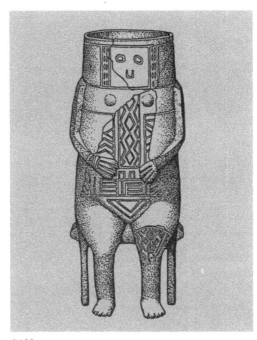

1432

Engravings on *1431*, a pottery figurine from the Theiss culture of Hungary, resemble mosaic garments. Note the knee-faces. Did knee-faces decorate high boots? A related example, *1432*, has eye-motifs at the knees.

Hocker-like figures on *1433*, an ancient
bronze halberd-blade from China or Indo-
China, have knee-faces.

A Greek Archaic greave, *1434*, circa
550–460 BC, is embossed & engraved with
a Gorgon, its eyes set with gems, its teeth &
tongue with ivory; while the classical
Greek greave in *1435*, from a statue of
Ares, simply has a Gorgon head on the
knee.

The artists who made these varied objects
left us no explanations of their intentions.
But underlying most of these examples, I
suspect, lies the fiction of male conception,
the knee being regarded as the true womb.

1433

1434

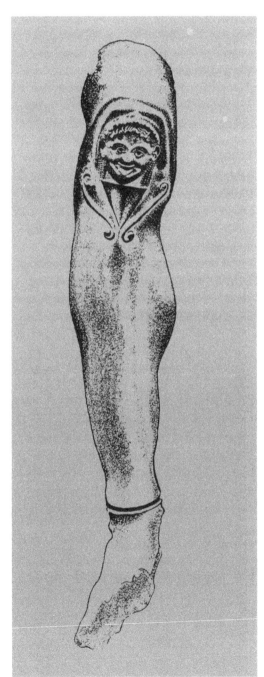

1435

Legitimation: Return to the Male Womb

In Yucatec, the word for *knee* also means 'head of lineage'; while in Mixtec, the word for *knee* also means 'womb' or 'umbilical cord'[184].

The name for 'knee' is used in the terminology of kinship throughout many languages, including all or most Indo-European languages. Many Indo-European terms for 'knee' are used alternately for ideas like 'degree of kinship' or 'generation'. Though the semantic connection is expressed variously in these different languages, all such variations can be traced back to the homonymy of two Indo-European roots: the nominal root *g'en* for 'knee' and the verbal root *g'en-*, which seems to mean 'beget'[185].

The homonymy of these roots leads to such correspondences as that between Latin *genu* for 'knee' and *genus* for 'descent'; Russian *kolieno* for 'knee' and the plural & distributive forms *koliena* & *pokolienie* for 'race', line, branch, stem, generation, degree of kinship; and the Irish use of *glun* for both 'knee' & 'generation'. There are similar correspondences in Germanic, Armenian, Persian, Sanskrit.

In Greek, the name for 'knee' appears to be cognate and sometimes interchangeable with 'generation'[186]. Euripides refers to knees as 'generative members'[187] and the knee is commonly referred to as the seat of paternity.

This knee-generation nexus seems basic in Indo-European languages. It occurs, as well, in Lapp and various Finno-Ungarian tongues[188]. Thus the Finnish *polvi* means both 'knee' & 'generation' and in the Finnish epic *Kalevala*, the sky-god Ukko generates three cloud-maidens when he presses his knee-cap[189]. For the Assyrians & Babylonians, whose language was unrelated to Greek or Latin, the word *birku* signified the knee or the male organ of generation[190].

In European lore & art, a departing son embraces his father's knees; a man thanking another clasps his benefactor's knees; and a captive begging for life clutches his captor's knees.

The Indo-European verbal root *g'en-*, meaning 'beget' (Latin *gigno*) is used to designate exclusively the parental role of the father, not that of the mother. This has been explained in terms of what appears to be a third homonymous root, *g'en-*, meaning 'know' (Latin *gnosco*). Meillet concluded that there was originally but one verbal root, meaning 'know' and that this came to mean 'beget' by being used in a special juridical sense: 'to know as ones own' or 'to recognize as legitimate', with a child as the implied object[191].

The Hebrew word for 'blessing' derives from the Hebrew for 'knee', in *Jeremiah* I,5, 'Before I formed thee in the belly I knew thee . . .'; the speaker is God and the word 'knew' is followed by 'sanctified' & 'ordained'.

From consideration of the Latin *genuinus*, meaning 'legitimate' (the u-stem of which marks it clearly as derived from the root for 'knee' and not from that for 'beget' or 'know'), Meillet & other linguists concluded that the homonymy of the roots for 'knee' & 'beget' rests, in the final analysis, upon the early existence of a rite of *legitimation or filiation* performed by the father, in which he recognized the newborn infant as his own by placing it upon his *knee*.

According to *Genesis* 48,12, Jacob considered Joseph's two sons, Ephraim & Manasseh, as his own and 'brought them out from between his knees'. 'And the children of Machir son of Manasseh were brought up upon Joseph's knees' (50,23).

Job, cursing the day of his birth, bewails the fact that he found two knees to receive him (3,12). From this, according to de Vaux, some authors concluded that childbirth sometimes took place on the knees of another person. 'But there is a simpler explanation: the texts . . . must be referring to adoption'[192].

Reminiscences of this custom persist at various levels of linguistic evolution in the Italo-Celtic & Indo-Iranian branches of the Indo-European family: in Germanic rites of adoption, which apparently involved placing a child upon the knee of its adoptive parent (presumably & properly its adoptive father); and in certain artistic traditions of early Christianity, eg *1436–1438*.

1436   1437   1438

In rural Ireland, until recently, when eldest sons delayed marriage until they inherited land, the resulting age-difference between spouses sometimes led to speculation about the legitimacy of children. A father might publicly declare his paternity by placing the infant on his knee.

This custom is specifically alluded to in Homer's *Iliad* (IX,455) and *Odyssey* (XIX,401). In Hesiod's *Theogony* (450) we are told that Kronos swallowed his children 'as soon as they came forth from the womb of their mother on to the knees'. There is no pronoun in the original specifying whose knees are meant, and this passage is generally translated with 'her' (ie the mother's) knees. But Benveniste convincingly supplies the masculine pronoun 'his', and infers that the children eaten by Kronos had been placed on his knees for the purpose of legitimation[193].

The tale of the father who devours each of his children as it is placed on his knee, seems to be a mythical projection of what *might happen* to children in the remote contingency that their father didn't 'recognize' them as his own, as sometimes happens under primitive economic conditions in Australia.

The Tupinamba custom of the father's (or natural uncle's) lifting the newborn from the earth[194] has a precise parallel in the Latin rite of *sublatio*, which, according to Loth, was the father's first act of recognition of the infant as his own: the father then placed the infant on his knees and named it, thus indicating that the child was not to be destroyed, but 'raised'[195].

Loth adds: 'The custom of placing the child on the ground seems to have been at first a type of homage to Mother Earth. It is on the ground as well that among Latins and Germans the dying were placed. The earth is the mother of men . . . : they come from her womb and they return there. The *sublatio* consequently appears to be a most general act involving the recognition of the child by the father'[196].

But the act of legitimation by lifting the child from the earth and placing it upon the father's knee was really *a symbolic return of the child to the place of its prior conception in the male*, and thus a repudiation of the conceptive role of the earth-womb.

Myths about the birth of the first human beings from the knees or, less specifically, from the legs of an Ultimate Ancestor occur in Africa, Asia & America, as well as in the 'Indo-European cosmology'. So the rite of legitimation may itself be rooted in a broad and presumably still more ancient mythical substratum. This rite, in which the father takes the new-born child upon his knee, then appears to be a re-enactment of the creation of the first human beings.

The Greek myth about the birth of Dionysos from the thigh of Zeus belongs to this class of legends, but it is far from 'primitive'. We are told that Dionysos was first conceived normally by a woman, Semele or Ge (probably 'Earth', who thus appears as a partner in a typical 'marriage of Heaven & Earth', but that the half-formed foetus, delivered prematurely from the mother's womb, was sewn by Zeus into his own thigh, where it remained until Zeus himself, upon its maturity, cut the binding threads and released the child[197]. A late 6th century BC amphora, *1439*, and a vase of circa 410 BC, *1440*, illustrate this event.

1439

1440

Couvade

Birth from limbs, legitimation, dismemberment & cannibalism all figure in this Greek myth of Dionysos. In Euripide's version, Pentheus is dressed up to impersonate Dionysos, then ritually dismembered & eaten, in particular by his female relatives.

The Greeks, I assume, recognized a relation between this tale and the *couvade*, known to them as a custom of their barbarian neighbors, for they poke fun at the Jovian childbed in their later comedies.

Undoubtedly there is such a relation. Yet the Greek myth hardly provides the best explanation of the *couvade*. It is atypical. No other myth about birth from legs mentions prior conception of the foetus in a woman's womb, or in fact makes any mention of normal birth whatever.

A better explanation of the *couvade* was given to a Portuguese voyager who visited the coast of Brazil in the 16th century. When Soares de Spisa asked a Tupinamba husband why he observed dietary & other typical restrictions of the *couvade* during the pregnancy & parturition of his wife, the man replied: 'because the child came out of his loins (*lombos*), and because all the woman can do is to guard the seed in the womb where the child grows'[198].

The distinction here is between planting & breeding. And it is this distinction which underlies the myth of the first birth from the 'legs' of a male ancestor. For the 'loins' of the Tupinamba male are functionally the same as the 'thigh' of Zeus.

The Greeks, by having Dionysos born first of a woman, were rationalizing an ancient legend, according to which Dionysos should have been born only from the leg of Zeus, and not from a woman at all. The Greek version violates the original conception.

This same tendency to rationalize the apparently irrational theme of first birth from the legs of a male ancestor may be seen in an African tale about a hero who 'slipped out of his mother's womb into her leg and was immediately full grown'[199].

What I regard as a rationalistic transfer from the knee to the vagina appears in a legend of one of the hill-tribes of India. According to this legend, 'originally the vagina was situated below the knee of the left leg. One day a chicken pecked at it, and it jumped up to a place of safety between the thighs, where it has remained ever since. But it was wounded, and blood flows from it every month'[200].

The epithets $\delta\iota\mu\dot{\eta}\tau\omega\rho$ & $\delta\iota\sigma\sigma\sigma\tau\acute{o}\kappa os$, meaning twice-born, applied to Dionysos, have their exact counterpart in the Sanskrit term, *dvijá*. This was applied to a man of any of the first three classes,

Rigveda X, who has been 'reborn' through investiture with the sacred thread. Was this thread equivalent to that with which Zeus sewed the immature foetus of Dionysos into his thigh in preparation for its 'second birth'?

The fantastic character of all such myths lies in the displacement of the supposed source of the 'seed' from the penis to the knee. The explanation may lie in the structure of certain genealogical patterns, eg 3. Here the heads of progeny occur 'on' the knees of their progenitors. A single figure, excerpted from such a pattern, often retains, between its knees & elbows, the heads of its two immediate descendants. Since such genealogical patterns were once the common property of much of mankind, this seems to me the most plausible explanation for the fact that, in widespread myths, the most commonly designated source of the 'first' children is the knees.

It is, after all, nothing but the actual physiology of procreation which many tribal peoples apprehend and then project symbolically in their tale of the 'first' birth from the legs of a male ancestor. Perhaps displacement of the 'seed' from a plausible penis to an implausible knee is felt to be appropriate to the supernatural character of this event.

The generative function of the knees is reflected in many myths & languages. The Yami of Botel Tobago say the penes of their progenitors were joined to their knees[201]. The Assyrians & Babylonians used a single word meaning both 'knee' & 'penis'[202]. This was also true in pseudo-Hittite[203]. These correspondences may be of the same order as the dual use of Latin *membrum* and German *Glied*, and the more recent jocular euphemisms for the penis such as 'third leg', 'short arm' & 'eleventh finger', the last recorded in Grimm[204].

This displacement from penis to knees hardly prevents us from recognizing that such myths attempt to explain an actual physiological process. 'Male birth' may strike us as a fantastic inversion of nature, and so it appeared to the rational Greeks who tried to set it right. But it is nothing but a figurative elaboration of one of the 'facts of life': the generation of semen in the male.

The Tupinamba's statement that 'the child came out of his loins', explains very well this myth about the birth of the first human beings from the 'legs' of a male ancestor. It also brings us as near as we shall probably ever get (and that is near enough) to the idea underlying the *couvade*. For this statement implicitly combines custom & myth in what must be their original & logical relation.

3

According to a Palaung tale from Burma, 'long, long ago . . . it was the man and not the woman who bore the children. The man carried the unborn child in the calf of his leg until the time when it was large enough to be born. . . . The man said . . . "Take the body and keep it warm in thy stomach. . . ." Then he saw that the woman had taken good care of the child . . . ; so, after that time, he gave over to the woman the care of the children.'[205].

Note the explicit priority of male over female birth, paralleling the Tupinamba explanation: the mother merely nourishes the child in her womb. This story also includes details (omitted from the above quotation) of an accompanying, and clearly symbolic transfer of the labors of fruit-gathering from the female to the male in exchange for her role in child-bearing. In the light of this tale, the *couvade* appears as a reversion to the original state of affairs, when men labored in child-birth and women in the production of food.

So much has been written, back & forth, about the custom of the *couvade* that it takes courage to attempt another generalization. Yet it seems to me that the statement of Tautain—remarkably brief for a communication on this subject— comes nearest the mark. He says that the basic motivation of the *couvade* must be the principle of *filiation* or *legitimation*: in other words, the recognition by the father that the child is really his, and an affirmation of his paternity[206].

The physiological relation of the child to its mother is proved by its birth from her body, but its relation to its father is not capable of equally ineluctable proof—a circumstance which has led to countless tragedies & comedies in real life & invention. To correct this inequity of nature, man provided his own means of establishing his paternity; and it is only natural, as Tautain says, that the rite by which he sought to establish it should be an imitation, or insofar as possible a counterpart, not to say an exaggeration, of the act by which woman gives birth.

This impulse adequately accounts for the drama surrounding the simulated parturition of the male, which has long fascinated scholars. All this drama is nothing but byplay to this basic idea, which is lost like the cloth under an elaborate embroidery.

Métraux doubted that the *couvade*, in South America, imitated childbirth[207]. I question this. The idea that the first 'womb' of mankind lay in the lap of a mythical male ancestor—an idea closely associated with the *couvade*—has an enormous distribution, including South America. And the common South American custom of the husband's 'keeping to his hammock' before, during or after his wife's parturition, surely imitates the woman's confinement. The same applies to food and other taboos observed by the husband, and sometimes by the wife.

Ultimately the idea expressed in the *couvade* is the priority of the male in the procreative process. On this priority is based the special relation between a father and his children manifested in the prohibition against the father's & children's eating each other in the 'creative' cannibalism of the Dieri & Aztecs. The Aztecs' justification of this abstention, 'Should I eat then of myself?', clearly derives from the idea that the child is 'born' first in the father.

The source of all these phenomena is the observation that the seed is generated in the male and only secondarily 'planted' in the female. What springs from such 'planting' is obviously that of the *sower*, the father. Undoubtedly it was a widespread sentiment which the Munurucu expressed when they described the role of the mother as being that of the earth: a seedbed[208].

Surely this explanation of the procreative process, with its analogy of the propagation of plants from seeds, accounts for the elaborate repudiation of the mother's role in the *couvade*. At the same time, it explains why the father & child are considered as one, regardless of the woman's intrusion. The mythological motif of the man's midwifery, practiced on his own leg or knee, is encountered not only in the Greek myth, but also in the myths of the African Masai, the Antillean Caribs and the Brazilian Umutina. Each asserts the spontaneity of the male procreative act—and of necessity symbolizes it in terms of childbirth from a woman.

This mythical midwifery is neither more nor less ridiculous than the man's behavior in the *couvade*; for the two are one. It is hardly surprising that this widespread idea crystallized in a special rite of filiation or legitimation, in which a father asserts his parentage by taking a new-born child upon his knee, as if it were the real 'womb' from which the child had come originally. Nor is it surprising that a memory of this rite is embodied in the very base of the Indo-European linguistic tree, in the homonymous roots for 'knee' & 'beget', which brings forth analogous fruits on various branches of that tree.

Couvade, myth, cannibalism, legitimation & language all perpetuate this one idea: an obsessive preoccupation with the special relation between father & child, based upon the prior activity of the father in the procreative process, and generally symbolized in a fictive male 'womb'. Perhaps even the exclusion of women from ritual life so commonly observed among tribal peoples throughout long phases of their social development is itself a reflection of this sentiment.

Colophon

The original print of Social Symbolism
was typeset in Sabon and printed via a
plate process at Meriden-Stinehour
Press in 1988. This is a digital color
reproduction optimized for spot printing
via print on demand of the original book with
new vectorized covers typeset in Sabon. The
project was led by Lorraine Spiess and
executed by Sofy Yuditskaya at
Edmund Carpenter's former office in
New York, New York, 2015.

Printed in the USA
CPSIA information can be obtained
at www.ICGtesting.com
LVHW070833051023
760132LV00013B/227